"Family trees are not 1 anything, they must be made up of stories, the ones that get passed down through the generations, and the ones that intrepid family researchers, like author Sherwood De Visser, are able to uncover. This book, *Raspberry Wars*, which is as heartwarming as it is heartbreaking, tells the stories of the thousand blooms on the author's amazing family tree—or perhaps, I should say a thousand and one, for like the tales of Scheherazade, these come straight from the heart of a gifted, natural storyteller."

Robert Hudson, author of *The Beautiful Madness of Martin Bonham, The Further Adventures of Jack the Giant Killer,* and *The Christian Writer's Manual of Style*

"What makes life bearable when other people, even relatives, fellow Christians, drive you into a corner? Is fighting back the best way? Sherwood De Visser explores this question thoroughly in his book about his and his mom's life. Read it! It will strike you as it struck me."

Dr. Jan P. Zwemer, author of *Van AIE, Zeeuws ABC,* and *van Zeeuws voor Beginners*

"*Raspberry Wars* is not merely a memoir about a mother who has all sorts of problems and her relationship with an adopted son, but a story of resilience, healing, and the power of ingrained Christian upbringing and love. De Visser is determined to break from the chains of family fights and bullying at home and in school, and reminds us that even the most fractured relationships can be repaired. Time, foundational principles learned indirectly through Christian practices at home, self-awareness, understanding, and the courage to find redemption in life—all contributed to his ability to overcome. It is a very inspirational story!"

Dr. Ray Vander Weele, author of *Stones that Speak*

"An insightful look back at generations past. De Visser's memories of traditional Dutch Reformed Church and school resonate with stories I've heard from forebears. We need to listen closely to voices like this from the pew sitter on the margins of polite society. De Visser's boyhood recollections are often painful, yet helpfully thought-provoking. Will we learn the right lessons from them, or continue our own little raspberry wars?"

Reverend Steven Hemmeke, pastor
Church of Christ, Howell, MI

"*Raspberry Wars* draws meaning from the lives of ordinary, imperfect folk. Exquisitely written, its beautiful storytelling set in historical events makes us feel—and wonder—What if? How? And why? *Raspberry Wars* brings the pattern and purpose of seemingly disparate events into a masterpiece of loving design. A wonderful, heartening read."

Maribeth Vander Weele, author of *The Joy of Job: An Investigator's Perspective on the Most Righteous Man on Earth*

"Is bullying just another inherent human trait exemplified by a child's 'innocent' cruel behavior or the abusive conduct of the power-enabled adult bolstered by a position of granted authority? Can it be prevented or controlled? Within this interesting auto-biographical tale, commencing from his days as an easy target of childhood bullies to his adult teaching position with an arguable responsibility to intervene, Mr. De Visser provides insightful views and conclusions on this timely topic. A fascinating, compelling, and thought-provoking memoir."

Roger A. Smith, Esq., Trial Attorney
Vandeveer Garzia, PC, Detroit, Michigan

"[Sherwood De Visser's memoir] of an abused childhood and uncertain identity in an oppressive atmosphere of small town religious hypocrisy [helped him find] redemption in the example of his grandmother's hard-earned wisdom. That is quite a story."

Dan Gerber, author of *Particles, Sailing through Cassiopeia, A Voice from the River,* and *Grass Fires*

RASPBERRY WARS

My Boyhood through Berries, Bullying, and Bravery

Sherwood
DeVisser

YOPI PRESS

Raspberry Wars: My Boyhood through Berries, Bullying, and Bravery

Copyright © 2023 by Sherwood De Visser
Yopi Press

All rights reserved. No part of this book may be reproduced or transmitted in any form or by any means, electronic or mechanical, including photocopying, recording, or any information storage and retrieval system, without written permission from the publisher.

Requests for information should be addressed to:
sherwooddevisser@gmail.com

This book is memoir. It reflects the author's present recollections of experiences over time. Some names and characteristics have been changed, some events have been compressed, and some dialogue has been recreated.

Trigger warning—this story describes bullying and contains references to emotional and sexual abuse.

Scripture quotations marked NLT are taken from the *Holy Bible*, New Living Translation, copyright © 1996, 2004, 2015 by Tyndale House Foundation. Used by permission of Tyndale House Publishers, Carol Stream, Illinois 60188. All rights reserved.

Scripture quotations marked CSB have been taken from the Christian Standard Bible®, Copyright © 2017 by Holman Bible Publishers. Used by permission. Christian Standard Bible® and CSB® are federally registered trademarks of Holman Bible Publishers.

Scripture quotations marked NIV are taken from the Holy Bible, New International Version®, NIV®. Copyright ©1973, 1978, 1984, 2011 by Biblica, Inc.™ Used by permission of Zondervan. All rights reserved worldwide. www.zondervan.com. The "NIV" and "New International Version" are trademarks registered in the United States Patent and Trademark Office by Biblica, Inc.™

Editor: Tisha Martin Editorial, LLC | www.tishamartin.com
Illustrator: Sara Hemmeke | www.sarahemmeke.com
Designer: Sarah Barnum | www.trail-blazes.com

Library of Congress Control Number:
ISBN: 979-8-9889115-0-0
E-book ISBN: 979-8-9889115-1-7

Printed in the United States of America

To school children everywhere.
May you find peace and hope in the journey
through your own raspberry wars.

CONTENTS

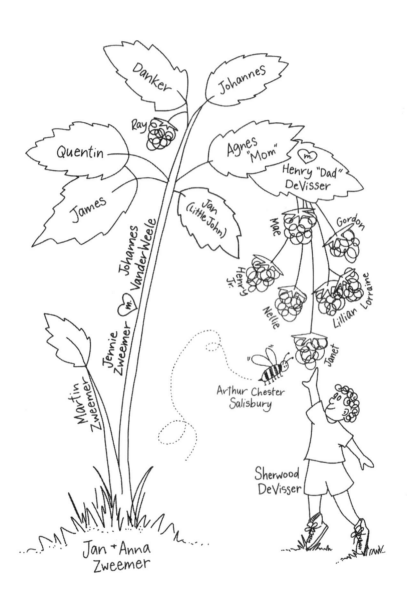

FOREWORD

In the history of Dutch migration to the United States, religion has been an important item, mentioned abundantly by many writers. However, the reasons for emigration recorded in Dutch municipal archives are described, in most cases, as "improvement of living conditions." Like most of the immigrants from other countries, many of the Dutch who ventured to wander westward and cross the Atlantic Ocean wanted a better life for themselves and their families. Their numbers: more than 200,000 between 1846 and 1914, and circa 100,000 during the years following the Second World War.

Especially during the Great Depression of Agriculture around 1880 and 1890, many fled from poverty at home. However, during an earlier wave of emigration, from 1846 to 1857, the religious factor had been more predominant. After the "Secession" in 1834, when the *Christelijke Afgescheiden Gemeenten* (Christian Seceded Congregations) split off from the old Dutch Reformed Church, the government applied a kind of soft oppression against these orthodox preachers and laymen. Many groups of Seceders, gathering around one of their ministers, settled in Michigan, Wisconsin, and Iowa. Some of the towns and villages there still honor their Dutch descent. The Christian Reformed Church is the heir of this Seceders' tradition. Others found their comfort in communities that gathered around the local Dutch Reformed Churches. Church life was important as religious identity mingled with the feeling of belonging to the Dutch nation. But from the First World War onward, this feeling dwindled in many of the immigrants and their children as they began to see themselves more and more just as Americans and nothing else.

This tradition and this tension can be seen in *Raspberry Wars*—but the story told here is much more than just a description of the Americanization of a Dutch family. The specific circumstances—time and place, the De Visser and Van der Weele families—form its real and determining background. But it is true: Dutch traits and orthodox Reformed features can be discerned in the people described. For example, the not touching of each other—not even the children—may be traced back to traditional agrarian society, at least in part.

In 1893, the Van der Weele family departed to the New World from the agrarian village of Nieuwdorp in Zeeland, one of the (at that time) eleven provinces of the Netherlands. That accounts, partially, for my relationship to this book and its author. As a historian, I am specialized in the nineteenth- and twentieth-century history of Zeeland agrarian society—religion, class relations, politics, and all that. My name, Zwemer, is nearly the same as that of Mrs. Van der Weele (Zweemer), but we are not closely related. My great-grandfather's uncle,

Adriaan Zwemer, immigrated to the USA in 1849, and during more than a century, my family at Oostkapelle, Zeeland, kept in touch with his descendants. In 1995, my friend Dr. James Kennedy, now Prof. Kennedy, gave me the opportunity to visit the USA and meet some of Adriaan Zwemer's descendants. James showed me the Midwest, where I visited Holland, Zeeland, Orange City, and many more places. When Sherwood De Visser describes the treeless landscape of western Iowa—well, I know it. I have been there, and it was a pleasure. Just like reading this book.

Dr. Jan P. Zwemer, freelance historian
Serooskerke, the Netherlands
July 2023

1

DO NOT PASS ME BY

Pass, me not O gentle Saviour, Hear my humble cry.
While on others Thou Are calling, Do not pass me by.

Fanny Crosby, Pass Me Not, O Gentle Saviour (1868)

wanted someone to protect me, but no one came, so I protected myself and tried to protect others. And the person I wanted more than ever to protect me was now dying. Up to that moment, I didn't give two hoots about understanding my family or their past, never asked the wherefores or how-comes. For who knows where and why and how come. It cannot be undone.

Now, as Mom lay dying, my past was going to the grave. I took her hand. *Don't let me stumble; don't let me fall, Mom. Let me talk with you. Lead me on, just hold my hand.*

I want to walk with you; I want to talk with you.

Mom rested, tightly tethered to hospital restraints in a circular bed of shiny steel with wires and tubes going in and out of her lungs, arms, and nose. She had been a bitter woman, but you couldn't tell it now. She had been a tormented soul, but it wasn't showing. In this bare, sterile white room overlooking Lake Michigan, she lay restrained and dying, but peaceable. She would no longer be falling down; I would no longer be picking her up. No more foaming at the mouth, no more horrid, ethereal cries into the air as she shook and convulsed and fell to the hard kitchen floor, or to the sidewalk, or in church in front of people who cared little about her.

No more screaming. Gone were the days not knowing up from down. Gone were the intense convulsions. The smile grew wider, but I knew she could not utter a word. She made a guttural sound or two like a baby's first attempt to talk. All that came out was babbling sounds. She struggled, sighed, then went still, and we just held hands. She attempted to make expressive faces all warming to me, yet it made me unable to hide my tears.

I think Mom had been vulnerable her entire life. Although she had epileptic seizures after I was born, it's unclear whether she had had any in her younger days. Now, to add to her sorrow-laden years, she was restrained in this hospital room to die. She still smiled. I didn't recall many occasions for smiles. But now she

16

smiled. Was it because she was drugged? Were her anti-epileptic medicines causing drowsiness and confusion? For years, these medications had attempted to control her seizures, but they had also slowed her cognition, fusing a dream state with reality. Though time and space collided, squeezing out all sense of reality, her eyes were bright and clear.

We held hands.

I could not recall holding her hand as a child, not in stores shopping, not for safety crossing the street, not for going into church on Sundays. As a child she never hugged me. Never voiced affection. But that might've been the Dutch way of things.

As a child, the closest I had ever gotten to loving embraces was being hoisted upside down and shoved into Dad's gritty face for goodnight whisker rubs. By bedtime, Dad's five o'clock shadow bore thickness and density that could sand off car paint, and a good rub back and forth reddened my baby soft cheeks, removing any skin imperfections I might have had. In an odd way, I enjoyed it, despite the burning sensation. Every night I anticipated the masochistic event as exhilarating and welcomed. It was the only kind of warm embrace I would ever receive.

I never gave Mom or the aunts any goodnight kisses or affectionate hugs. Nor were there any overtures by them to welcome one. Any other touching came in the form of red welts from my aunt Lorraine's finger claws, with some good pinching on my bare arms, and on occasion, a bit of bloodletting as she beat me about the head and face.

There Mom and I sat together, waiting for the Lord to come along. We continued to touch, her eyes bringing up soft smiles I had not seen before. Maybe she was searching for a silver lining in the clouds.

We had fought so much during my teen years that I couldn't recall a peaceful moment until now, as she lay on her deathbed. And our confrontations couldn't be quantified. It wasn't about my maturation in adult-hood or my rebellion for being adopted, as other family accused me of whenever there was a familial dispute. The fights grew out of nothing and because of noth-ing, at least on my part. It wasn't pretty. Me pushing the boundaries of civility and shouting at her, and her shouting back and throwing ashtrays, salt and pepper shakers, a kitchen fork or bread knife—whatever was in arm's reach. I can't process those many episodes with-out feeling ashamed and deeply saddened.

I couldn't do anything but be in full contrition. I felt I let had her down. It wasn't for ignorance that I became disrespectful, for I damn well knew of her multiple maladies; I simply made myself a social martyr. I should have understood her disabilities, been more patient, been a good child, been respectful and honor-ing to her and Dad. They took me in when I could have ended up in a barren foster system. It wasn't until I was grown that I learned that my "sister" Janet was actually my biological mother and the woman I knew as "Mom" was actually my maternal grandmother. Following the unfortunate circumstances of my birth, Mom raised me as her own.

Mom had a hard life, first of laborious tedium caring for her parents and her five older brothers, then later living with disappointed hopes for her marriage and family, which went sideways. Mom had epilepsy for most of her life, a disease which was misunderstood by most folks. She never mentioned anything about her seizures. Actually, she never mentioned anything about her childhood growing up in Sheboygan, Wisconsin. Never did she voice fond memories of doing girlfriend things. No mention of lost loves or silly boyfriends in school. Regarding social interactions as a young girl, she was mute. The way soldiers coming back from war never talked about those dark experiences, Mom never spoke of childhood but once—a tale of her and her brother Danker "burning down an orchard." No details, that was all.

I imagined Mom as a kid experiencing a grand mal seizure in front of her classmates. It would have been psychologically and socially disastrous. Mom's seizures lasted up to three minutes. As a child, it was my job to remove Mom's dentures during an epileptic episode. When her false teeth flopped around inside her mouth, they could choke her. A person could also swallow his or her tongue, choking off the air supply. That might be a myth now, but back then, we knew it to be true. My hands were quick, and I could reach into her mouth and pull out her dentures without losing my fingers, before she bit through her tongue or cheek. I was kid quick. I could catch crayfish, snakes, and once, at the age of five, I caught a fox squirrel by its tail as it came down a tree.

I know Mom thought the Lord kindled His anger on her, and the church's tenets certainly enabled that sad thought to worm into her thinking. Our faith taught that a downturn in health or wealth was a warning, the Lord sending a message to the unfortunate receiver to mend their ways. You could read the New Testament parable where Jesus cast out demons and sent the "legion" into the herd of pigs, and easily reason that the suffering person needed exorcism. The sinner needed to perform deep introspection, and upon finding the calamitous sin, repent. Surely, that was the remedy for sins a tier below an abomination. Sincere repentance could be measured by gaining back one's health or wealth, and then the church congregants could sigh with relief and gossip over luncheons with spiritually upright friends that the sinner was back in the fold. Although demon possession was not contagious, you could never be too careful.

Those floral dresses were now replaced by a white hospital gown. Trying not to choke up, I looked deep into her eyes. It was the first time I recognized that she had hazel eyes. Her hair, always tucked tight under a hair net, now fell gracefully around her face. Mom's brightening spirit shone while we held hands, our first outward sign of embracing emotion in a nonviolent manner. At that moment, Mom and I worked out our differences. She loved me in her own way. Ours was a soft, spiritual touching, her smiling eyes telling me we were okay. Her sorrowful soul was moving on. She was going home.

Leaving her bedside, I approached a couple of nurses, who said that she really perked up when she saw me. They said she had been quite peaceful the last couple of days, free from argument or violent conflict. That was not Mom. It had to be the drugs. But they said there had been no change to her medications.

In all the years of her possible unbelief that the Lord didn't love her, I believe in this instant she held hope the Lord would not pass her by. But before going home, she made things right for me. I hope I did the same for her. That evening, after I had to leave, she slipped away. Her wandering soul went home. The demons of epilepsy left her to find another to torment.

Mom died alone in Traverse City State Hospital, an institution for the psychologically insane. Our small town of Fremont, and especially her church, did not know who Mom really was, who she had been as a young woman. They did not know her family history, and had they, there would have been more compassion, I suspect.

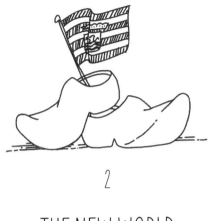

2

THE NEW WORLD

The Dutch do have a slightly odd sense of humor.

Bill Bailey

Mom's parents were Johannes Van der Weele and Jennie Zweemer, both of Dutch extraction, born and raised in the Zeeland Province of the Netherlands. Jennie's father, Jan Zweemer, had started as an unskilled laborer, working on the polders and dikes. He worked his way up, learning the business of hydro engineering (draining water from the North Sea and developing fertile, arable farmland). By age twenty-nine, he had secured a lucrative contract from the Dutch government.

Jan Zweemer was one of the most important men in the Zeeland Province, responsible for the care and maintenance of thirty-six polders, powerful windmills screws that churned out North Sea water next to dikes capable of holding back the North Sea from literally washing away the quaint Zeeland villages and farms he had created from a chain of islands called an isthmus. This impressive hydro engineering feat can be seen by comparing seventeenth-century maps of the Zeeland Province with late nineteenth-century maps in an atlas. What were once unconnected islets became a peninsula, and with it came a proud, independent spirit of pious Dutch Protestants. Their ancestors had won independence from the Spanish Catholics and the Holy Roman Empire in the Eighty Years' War of the sixteenth century, ushering in a Golden Age for the Dutch. And pride fully so, as succeeding generations were winning the war against nature and her fickle sea.

Jan Zweemer passed away suddenly at a young but undetermined age. Village officials were at his bedside when he died. He left his wife, Anna, and his children, Martin and Jennie, with substantial earnings that allowed them to live well, keep the fine house, and purchase a farm in Nieuwendorp, Zeeland. Jennie married Johannes Van der Weele, a common farm laborer, who possibly worked for Jennie's father. In 1880, the United States flooded the European market with cheap grains, which collapsed the Dutch agribusinesses for decades. The economic conditions deteriorated so much that there were food riots in Amsterdam. By 1893, with the

Netherlands still deep in economic malaise, there was not much of a bright future left for my maternal great grandparents. Jennie's mom, Anna, needed more care. The inheritance had dwindled, making it difficult to keep the farm going since Dutch wheat was no longer a profitable commodity, and jobs were scarce for unskilled laborers like Johannes.

On March 1, 1893, Johannes and Jennie boarded the *SS Nieuw Amsterdam* ocean liner at the port docks of Rotterdam, Netherlands, and immigrated to America.

Martin Zweemer, Jennie's brother, whom I knew as Uncle Martin, had already set out to America in 1892 and settled near Sheboygan, Wisconsin. He bought land and began to farm. Uncle Martin kept Jennie up to speed with numerous letters of encouragement. Martin convinced the family to embark for America, and he would act as sponsor. They should have no problems; America would welcome them, he assured.

For Jennie, her priority for the voyage was keeping the children healthy and, hopefully, her mother, Anna, alive. Ship travel was grueling and dangerous crossing the fickle Atlantic Ocean, and this was Jennie's main worry. Sea travel was the only option in those days, and since health and living conditions were rough, many small children under the age of two perished on these ocean voyages.

Uncle Martin instructed the family to take only essentials, no sentimental family artifacts. As was Dutch nature, Jennie was a pragmatic woman. She and Johannes geared up and set about getting provisions, as advised. Johannes procured potatoes, buckwheat flour, beans, dried meat, bacon, pepper, salt, vinegar, coffee, and especially tea. Jennie didn't know exactly why Uncle Martin had said "especially tea," but she respected his advice and complied.

Jennie had Johannes purchase a small vat of salted fish from the market and also a small vat with a spigot that could be used to get their daily supply of water, instructing Johannes to fill it before they left. The family packed few clothes. Carrying over a hundred pounds worth of clothing would cause extra charges. Jennie packed smaller trunks that Johannes could handle. She went to the baker and purchased some rye and wheat bread and sliced the loaves thick to let them dry. All this would amount to two hundred pounds of food to feed them aboard the ship.

The ocean voyage would be long, but their prayers to their sovereign God would see them safely through. Jennie had faith in the sovereignty of God and prayed daily. Jennie did stowaway some non-essentials: her church books, one Bible, and one New Testament— essentials in her mind.

They boarded the *Nieuw Amsterdam* and set out.

They watched from the ship's deck as Rotterdam's numerous windmills shrank behind, in front of them a watery horizon west across the Atlantic to New York

City. When the land was out of view and gray waters were all they could see, the families would be permitted to continue to walk on the outer decks if the weather was mild. Nineteenth century sailing ships took a minimum of two to three weeks to cross the Atlantic. With the ill-tempered Atlantic and hostile winds and concurrent bad weather generally associated with early spring, the journey could take up to fourteen weeks, with the sails down since they were heading directly into the westward winds.

Jennie recalled seeing a copper/brass sign on the ship that read: *Willen De Scheepsgezllen Zich Onthoudn Van Het Urinenen Vanaf Het Potten Eu Pannendek.* Translated in English: "Will Members of the Crew Kindly Refrain from Urinating on the Poop Deck." Apparently, defecation was already understood by the deckhands to be verboten, despite the deck's name. When not on deck catching fresh air, the family was quartered in Spartan conditions in the belly of the ocean liner toward the rudder and engine area. Noisy, damp, and compartmentalized by class, my maternal great grandparents lived for the duration of the voyage.

Johannes and Jennie had never traveled outside of the delta region of the Zeeland Province. They had no idea what life would be like on an immigrant ship in the late nineteenth century, particularly among the working-class passengers known as "steerage class." They would have to live below deck in the steerage area by the screws and propeller where it was dark, damp, cramped, and often crawling with rats. Lice, ticks, and cockroaches were also fellow passengers.

Poor hygiene made things worse for the steerage class. There would be problems with the toilets and the pipes would be choked, and, consequently, disease would become prevalent. This led to outbreaks of serious diseases like scarlet fever, typhoid, smallpox, measles, and diphtheria. The youngest passengers were the hardest hit. Danker, then Jennie's youngest at six months old, may have taken ill because years later, when retelling of the voyage, claimed he survived not only by the grace of God, but also by his mother feeding him barley bread dipped in tea.

However, immigrant passenger ships were not always disease-ridden. Many of the Dutch immigrants were a higher working-class group of people. In addition, if the ship struck good weather most of the voyage, the passengers would not fare too badly at all. For Johannes and Jennie, it was uncomfortable and laborious, cramped, and probably claustrophobic, but the weather held, and their voyage was shorter.

They arrived to New York, New York safe and intact. A reassuring sign, the Statute of Liberty. My cousin Ray Vander* Weele, who grew up knowing

* *The historic Van der Weele name was later changed to Vander Weele (no space between Van der) by some family members.*

Jennie, stated that Jennie, upon arriving in New York, was excited to see the Statue of Liberty. However, she noticed that the Statue of Liberty had its back turned on Ellis Island. A peculiar and humorous observation, we thought.

Before being processed at Ellis Island, the ship docked at New York proper, since the first- and second-class passengers were excluded from immigration regulations and didn't have health inspection. It was assumed by the New York port authorities that these folks, since they had enough money to be first- and second-class passengers, were disease free. Once these passengers disembarked, remaining passengers boarded ferries to Ellis Island. Port authorities pinned a slip of paper to their clothes indicating the ship manifest on which their names would be found, and then they were made to walk single file through the Ellis Island entrance doors.

Upon entering the building, they would be confronted by a young, hard-faced man in military uniform, the United States Public Health Service physician, who was undergoing training as a line inspector at Ellis Island. Every man, woman, and child was made to walk past him and be assessed for physical and mental defect. Once Johannes and Jennie and the kids passed that inspection, they turned the corner and faced another physician, older and more experienced, who quickly marked in chalk any immigrant suspected of disease or defect.

The immigration process was unremarkable for them since everybody was healthy, and Anna Zweemer was, as Johannes explained in Dutch, a *"taaie oude vogel"* (tough old bird). And although Johannes was a low-skilled laborer, the US government knew that the Dutch immigrants assimilated better into the American way and exclaimed that they would be "productive sober citizens in quick time." And with Uncle Martin sponsoring them and producing evidence that he had already rented a home for them near Oostburg, Wisconsin, Jennie and family were deemed clean and acceptable to enter America.

After the family arrived at the New York port, it was the travel from Buffalo, New York, through the Great Lakes and beyond that was the most perilous part of the journey, as many Dutch and other immigrants would discover. Steamship voyages along the Great Lakes had a history of frequent disasters. In actuality, some 6,000 shipwrecks were recorded on the Great Lakes, including 1,600 on Lake Michigan and 1,000 off Saginaw Bay on Lake Huron. Best known to the Dutch was the infamous voyage of *The Phoenix*, which sank just within sight of Sheboygan shores. An entire Dutch congregation disappeared under the merciless gray waters of Lake Michigan.

Johannes and Jennie Van der Weele arrived safely in Oostburg, Wisconsin, began their new life in the New World, and, according to the 1910 United States

Census, became productive, sober, and anglicized. Johannes found work as a dipper in a coaster wagon shop in Oostburg. Jennie successfully birthed three more healthy boys: John, Quentin, Johannes, and one daughter, the youngest, Agnes. My cousin Ray used to say that these people formed the "branches and twigs" of the Johannes and Jennie Van der Weele family, which shaped my world.

By 1924, Jennie's sons had married and started new families. Only Agnes (my maternal grandmother) remained home to care for her now-aging parents in Sheboygan, Wisconsin. There she became keeper of the garden out back, which also included a chicken coop and a large linear raspberry patch.

3

UNCLE MARTIN

Don't trust the preachers in Holland, Michigan—a greedy lot.

Peter Zonne

I f it had not been for Martin Zweemer, the first Van der Weele to come to America, Jennie would not have gathered up her three children and moved. If it were not for Peter Zonne, Uncle Martin would not have settled in the Wisconsin area.

When Peter Zonne immigrated to the US in 1847, he had heard reports of sickness and hardship in the Holland, Michigan, colony of Dutch immigrants. Additionally, Peter had been warned that the Dutch ministers in Holland, Michigan, were a rather greedy lot. Reports had come out that the Dutch ministers controlled the buying and selling of land in the congregation's colony. If the people made a profit from land sales, they would have to turn it over to their ministers. This was a law passed by the ministers—one of many that seemed designed to get money out of the pockets of Dutch congregants. It was not the law of the land. Greedy ministers had been a catalyst for Dutch Protestants and friends to leave the Netherlands in addition to the wheat market crisis. Peter once said that the ministers were even worse in Holland, Michigan, than they were in the Netherlands.

Peter selected instead an area near the port of Sheboygan, Wisconsin, where a friend of his had already settled. It was through Peter that Uncle Martin would also come to settle there. Like Peter, Uncle Martin felt ordinary American laws were good enough for him, and he once told Jennie, "I came here to be free and not be ruled by tyrants again. The ministers come to America to get rich and make servants of us innocent and simple-minded Dutch immigrants."

Sheboygan was not the same way. It wasn't a Dutch enclave but primarily a colony of German Catholics. Martin held no fear of the Catholics having possible adverse influences on the increasing Dutch population there. He may have forgotten the story of Catholic oppression upon the Dutch centuries before. He may have not been listening.

Uncle Martin purchased parcels of virgin Wisconsin forest and cut and cleared and hauled the lumber to the port of Sheboygan for extra cash. He also worked in a sawmill to support his family. He rented an eighty-acre farm on a seven-year lease, cleared twenty acres, and was able to pay rent by selling lumber from the land not cleared. He would occasionally hire himself out to other neighboring farmers as well. He prospered. He thanked the Lord for sending him to North America because it was a land that was blessed and abundant. He continued to work hard and save money and was able to buy another 160 acres of land by the time he sent a letter enticing Jennie to set out for America.

When he retired in 1934, Uncle Martin decided to take a trip back to the Old Country to visit relatives and see how things had changed or stayed the same. He traveled throughout the small Dutch land, and when he returned to Sheboygan, he wrote his observations in a detailed narrative, which was published by the *Sheboygan Press*.

Two things struck him. First was the change in the religious climate. The Dutch were rejecting their Reformed faith, a shocking turn, he said, which wouldn't bode well for the future he felt. Losing one's religion was bad enough on an individual level, but as a country, that was unsettling. He prophesied ill times for the Netherlands. It seemed the Dutch were lured to the siren call of socialist ideals that already had spread across Western Europe, most prominently in Germany, Netherland's major neighbor. His second observation came when he traveled to the German/Dutch border. At the bridge at *Nijmegen,* he noticed a brand-new highway system coming from Germany, butting up to the Dutch border. He traveled to several other Dutch/German border cities and noticed the same thing: new road systems all leading from Germany to the Dutch border. But there was no traffic on these highways.

In his narrative for the Sheboygan paper, Uncle Martin asserted that the German Chancellor was planning on invading the Netherlands. The German Chancellor he named was Adolf Hitler. At the time his article was written, FDR's administration put glowing and inspiring faith in Hitler and "the good he was doing for the German unemployed," according to Martha Eccles Dodd, daughter of then US Ambassador William Dodd. Martha Dodd—who at the time was in numerous sexual liaisons with high-ranking Germans, including Rudolf Diels, the director of the Gestapo.

In 1893, Jennie and the kids had joined Uncle Martin along the shores of Lake Michigan next to the coal yards of its shipping port. The Van der Weeles survived a smallpox epidemic, learned English, and got along with their German neighbors, and were allowed to seek employment, obtaining jobs at Kohler, a German manufacturing plant. The workers became known as "kohlers."

At age nineteen, Mom secured a job at Kohler and worked there for years. Time moved as time does, and

Mom found herself at age thirty, still living at home and working for Kohler, unmarried and looking for love.

4

THE STRANGER COMETH

Hold the agitated, secular world at arm's length,
not putting faith in earthly powers, but in Christ's powers.

Dr. Stephen Vander Weele

Mom was handed off to a stranger. She said he was from the Old Country like her family, from the Zeeland Province "like us." That's what he said in *The Banner*, the Dutch denomination's church magazine, when he advertised for a housekeeper. No one knows who responded, whether Mom, her dad, or Jennie, but a responsive letter was sent to one Henry De Visser of Lester, Iowa.

Mom was dancing around spinsterhood, turning thirty. She was reaching spinsterhood or, probably in her dad's eyes, had already been ensconced in spinsterhood.

For Mom, time was catching up, and she possibly felt she could not live with her parents much longer. She had a life to lead too. Regardless of who answered the advertisement, the stranger was now coming up from Lester, Iowa, to take a gander at this Agnes Van der Weele.

It may have been a familial conscription. Perhaps Mom's parents felt an urgency to answer the ad and point out the positive possibilities for Agnes. The pool of eligible men in Sheboygan was small, and there were very few prospects in her neighborhood. The best Dutch men were married by age twenty. The Germans were out because they were Catholic and drinkers. She was surrounded by a large Catholic community, and that would not suit well to marry a Catholic. Nice folks, but not interested in intermarrying in those days.

The irony is that a generation later, my mom's nephew, Ray Vander Weele, would marry Phillis, a Roman Catholic, and have a dual religious wedding ceremony. But back in the early twentieth century in Midwest America, Roman Catholics and Protestants didn't intermarry. No devout Catholic priest or Protestant preacher would have done such a mixed religious ceremony.

Time was a cruel mistress, and Mom had to be aware of the ticking of the biological clock and the fragility of life. The Van der Weeles lived near the Catholic cemetery, where funerals occurred every day. The horse-drawn hearse moved up the block toward the expansive Catholic cemetery with its idolatrous icons of saints and some sinner. Lavish mausoleums, crypts, and sepulcher vaults, adorned in Italian marble, showed even the rich were to die.

The daily imagery of the passing of life embedded in her an acute knowing that Sheboygan was a dying planet, inescapable, the reality of death striking home, especially when she knew many Catholics as neighbors and distant acquaintances.

For years she had prayed for a new beginning, and maybe this is what the Lord wanted. Of course, a husband was what she had hoped for, not an employer. But at least he was her kind of people. Henry De Visser was forty-one and had been born in Colinsplaat, Zeeland, Netherlands, just a biking distance from Nieuwdorp, the Van der Weele village. Mom had never been there, knew nothing of there, except what Jennie had passed on to her. Flat farmland, beneath sea level. Of polders and earthen dikes holding back the tempestuous North Sea. Since Agnes had been born in Sheboygan, her mother's stories of the Old Country were just that. Stories.

The only significant difference was that the stranger was a Reformer and not a Christian Reformer, which she felt at ease about, to a point. "A loosening of orthodoxy, but not by much," said Father. Now they were just woozy, singing hymns instead of the Psalms. That's all. His response soothed her. Daughter Agnes needed a change. What would Henry look like? Although he had sent a picture, he was still coming to interview her for a job.

And that's the way it was. That's the way it would be. The stranger was coming to take her away to be a caretaker and housekeeper in Iowa.

She'd be leaving Sheboygan, the only home she knew. She would be leaving her five brothers, whom she loved. The brothers' frozen work slacks on the clotheslines would now be replaced by this stranger's family's clothes.

She'd miss walking the cold concrete pier in the upper harbor, the piercing foghorn off Lake Michigan just beyond the quarry. She'd miss tending her mother's garden and listening to the long wail of the train whistle of the Chicago Northwestern Railroad about 5:45 in the evening. Rarely did it arrive even a few minutes late, and when it did, the editor of the *Sheboygan Press* would make note of it in his editorial page. Gone would be picking the beans, the beets, and the raspberries, a disciplined and monotonous labor that was meditative to her.

And she'd miss the streetcar she would take to work to the Vollrath-Kohler manufacturing plant at the city's far limits. She loved the streetcar ride. It gave her time to sit and rest.

Her mother had taught her how to hold the agitated secular world at arm's length, not putting faith in earthly powers but in Christ's orders, submitting to the flamed earthly authority when appropriate. Jennie had stated,

"We live in God's time and in God's sight, but we have to obey earthly powers."

Mom had no real friends in church save her five brothers. Yet for her, church in general held a special place because it linked her to European communities that she had never seen but that her parents had brought to America.

Mom attested that she lived in God's time. That's what mattered. Obedience to God and honoring one's parents. Now she was carving out a new life in a new world called Iowa, away from Kohler factory work sixty hours a week, away from worldly amusements of Sheboygan of which she had not been allowed to partake. Away from the taverns, which she avoided but her Catholic neighbors unabashedly attended. Away from the dance halls, Mother's strictly forbidden place, and away from any possible temptation to a mixed marriage with German Lutherans or German Catholics. Such unions would compromise their faith and even their eternal soul. Parents had ingrained in their children scary anecdotes akin to the Brothers Grimm tales. The broad road leads to destruction. Narrow is the path that leads to life. Away into a farming life.

Agnes said she was tending her parents' raspberry patch when the stranger arrived.

Her father peeked out the front window and witnessed a bright green Chevy Coach with black-and-white Iowa plates parking curbside.

"That's a new car," said Johannes.

Jennie muttered, "Prideful . . . a new car."

"Now stop that," said Johannes, closing the curtain and calling for Agnes.

Agnes stood from her garden toil, straightened out her dress, and walked into the house.

5

A LAND THAT TIME WON'T COMMAND

To the ends of the earth, will you follow me?
There is a world to follow that was meant for ours to see.

Ben Schneider

Henry De Visser needed help desperately. He was unmarried, taking care of his aging parents as his five brothers and one sister had all gone off and married, leaving him alone with his mercurial father and sick mother. Within the first week of his visit to Sheboygan, Henry changed his plan. He took a liking to Mom. As the story was told to me, Henry De Visser set to stay a week to bring back a housekeeper but stayed a month and brought back a wife.

Henry courted Mom for a month, and after many

opportunities to get to know each other (under strict supervision by her brothers and parents), he asked for Mom's hand in marriage. Mom thought him handsome and took a liking to his endearing mannerism. He spoke little but held a soft smile. He was not bombastic. He was respectful to her parents.

A small wedding was held, Agnes in a light blue wedding dress and Henry in a dark formal suit. Mom's youngest brother, "Little John," was best man, and his wife, Lena, was matron of honor. Did Agnes feel like dancing, drifting to music playing out into a prairie harvest moon? Was she flowing where two rivers diverged, one away from the sea, the other to the Great Divide? Was this falling in love? Were they going to be lovers bound in blissful celebration? Was love getting a hold on her? She was more than a creation; she was a new woman. And this stranger wanted her!

Mom packed up with this stranger, leaving her safe world. What were her thoughts? What must she have felt? How did she feel going to the ends of the earth? And running a farm, to boot. Mom later confessed she had had no concept of Lester, Iowa. It was as foreign as Nieuwdorp and Colinsplaat, Netherlands. The green Chevy Coach with Iowa plates IA-2851 left Sheboygan, Wisconsin, and headed west, out of view of her parents.

I often wondered how that departure transpired. Happy fanfare? Perhaps hugs, soft admonishments, and instructions from Jennie, who knew all about going to a new world. Did Johannes shake Henry's hand? Mom's brothers didn't particularly care for Henry, especially Mom's favorite brother, Danker. Did her family pray for her prosperity? Did the Christian Reformer congregation give her a blessing? Did Jennie hug Mom as Johannes and Henry packed the motorcar? And as the fancy, shiny car pulled away from the Lincoln Street house, did Jennie and Mom shed tears? Perhaps Jennie admonished her daughter to write often. Maybe one last loving embrace from parents, humorous chiding by her brothers, a promise to visit her often. Or, quite possibly, knowing our Dutch culture, a prickly and stately goodbye sufficed.

The green motorcar pulled away on a quiet April day. The grand Dutch elms of Sheboygan faded behind as the great prairie came into view. The car passed the city limits and headed southwest down Highway 151, Dubuque-way, as Mom quietly thanked God for this man. The Lord was filling her with anticipation, hope, and a new relationship. Now, not a stranger. Not her employer but a new friendship. Her husband, a handsome one at that. He had strong hands and high cheekbones with deep eyes. Strong as the Belgian plow horses he bridled and plowed across sixty acres of deep, rich soil.

Her humble life now handed over to this man in this shiny green car, Mom felt blessed for moving above her station. Henry was a strong man; she would be secure, well cared for, and blessed at last. She hadn't had an epileptic seizure since he had come to Sheboygan. Something she never thought would be her lucky lot. As the sun rose in the sky, her spirits did fly.

With trees and the Great Lake left behind, Mom cozied up to her Henry. Tulips and raspberries were replaced by pink prairie smoke flowers, whispering into her heart. The sunsets were different, brilliant cascading colors portending good things. She had never seen sunsets like this before, where the sun seemed to take its time before bringing on night's cold. She was becoming a wayfaring gypsy girl, vanishing toward a whole wide land, to its setting sun and its tall grasses where time wouldn't command.

She had followed Henry to the sun, followed to where it sets, to the end of the Earth.

Mom rarely spoke of that new home. She spoke of the farm and the animals on the farm. By 1933, she had a flock of sheep. Henry carried on the difficult outdoor farm duties, plowing with Belgian draft horses, one named Princess. But Mom uttered little about the house.

Mom's in-laws, Garrett and Maatje, didn't want to share their rooms with her. Garrett verbally abused Mom. He darkened Mom's brightening new world. She started this new life with the hope of a future family, a new beginning, a new meaningful thing to give her purpose in her Christian life, but Garrett drew upon his sins and splashed despair on Mom.

Nevertheless, as she set out for a new meaning of Christian hope and faith in what Jesus wanted for her and her life, her spirit radiated with faith sustainable. Her express purpose now was to seek joy and relationship with her man, Henry, and create a new family.

6

ARRIVAL

They will fade away like a little flower in the field. The hot sun rises and the grass withers; the little flower droops and falls, and its beauty fades away.

James 1:10–11 (NLT)

Mom spoke little of her new home. She rarely voiced anything about the early years of her life with Dad. It must have been a tough life, living on the Great Plains away from her extended family roots. Dad bought Mom two wedding presents: a Victor Orthophonic Victrola, the first consumer phonograph player designed specifically to play electronically recorded phonograph records, and a beautiful oak dining table.

And although living on the Great Plains at that time was a tough life for young women, that first year, Mom and Dad seemingly had fun, listening to music and maybe evening going to dances. I have in my possession that Victor Orthophonic Victrola, along with Mom's hundred or so 78 RPM vinyl records. Her 78s collection was jazz, swing, dance band, and ragtime. Despite living a hard life farming, making babies, and caring for Dad's aging parents, in all estimation, Mom and Dad were having fun. Dad bought a new Indian motorcycle, and I was told he had been in a jazz band near Rock Valley, Iowa.

Mom adjusted to Iowan farm life out on the northwest plains. It was more drastic weather than in Sheboygan. Snow drifts could be as high as barn roofs, and Mom found herself shoveling paths from the house to the barn to feed the sheltered animals and her beloved flock of sheep. She got used to the flat land and no trees, which she found unsettling, but Dad pointed out that you could see the tornadoes twelve miles out, giving the farmers time to shelter their horses and kids. The cattle were left to their own devices. I recall hearing stories about tornadoes picking up cattle and sucking them into the debris-filled funnel cloud, the helpless cows bellowing to a looming demise.

Within the first year of marriage, Mom bore a baby girl and named her Mae. She lived a week. After losing baby Mae, Mom bore a second baby girl in February 1931, nine months later. She gave the baby the same name as her first child, according to Dutch tradition. Mae was healthy and had a ruddy complexion and grew strong.

But she was not what Dad wanted or needed: he needed boys. He was tiring of working the farm alone, and girls were an additional burden.

He kept trying. Mom kept birthing girls. By 1936, incredibly, Mom had borne four sets of fraternal twins— two sets of stillborns and two sets of healthy girls. Somewhere in that menagerie of babies, Mom finally bore Dad a son. A namesake son, Henry De Visser, Jr.

Between pregnancies, Mom continued to care for her in-laws, Garrett and Maatje, two sober and humorless individuals. According to sparse anecdotes I heard from family members, Garrett and Maatje were mean, cold, and unwelcoming toward Mom. Garrett was seemingly against the hasty marriage from the get-go, against Dad leaving the farm for a month, and against this spinster woman he brought back not as a housekeeper but as a new member of the family. Even upon his deathbed, as Mom lovingly cared for him, cleaning, bathing, and feeding him, Garrett verbally abused her— relentlessly I'm told.

Dad's siblings were kind and accepting. He had ten siblings (three named Wilhelmina, who all died before their first birthdays), but when the family immigrated to America, only five siblings came with their parents: Pietrenella, Ary, Adriaan, Isaac, and Dad. (For whatever reason two of the siblings stayed in the Netherlands.) Dad was the youngest and, according to Mom, the most handsome of the brothers.

After the family arrived in America, Dad lived on his parents' large farm. Isaac started his own farm close by, Ary moved to Holland, Michigan, and Adriaan moved to California, becoming a speculator of land in the Castro Valley and Palto Alto regions. He became rich, then his wife died, and shortly thereafter he married the nurse caretaker, thirty years his junior. That was the summer of 1955.

Mom loved Adriaan. He was so full of life. When she first met him, she admired his outlook and "go git 'em" visionary outlook. He and Dad held the same daring spirit—Dad by participating a jazz band, riding his Indian motorcycle, and operating a large farm; Adriaan by seeking fortune in distant California and succeeding. Mom rarely spoke of Dad's other brothers, Isaac and Ary. They were hardworking fellows but didn't seem to have the daring spirit that Dad and Adriaan possessed.

Mom got along with Pieternella the best, and when I knew "Aunt Nellie," she was fun-loving and possessed a wry sense of humor. I enjoyed her immensely. Even though she was an old woman and I was an excitable boy, we found common ground in looking at life humorously. She had had to use a cane, made from oak with a shepherd's hook. When I teased her, she would flip the cane around, hook my legs or waist, and pull me to her with a smile, and we laughed together. It was our game.

But as Providence would have it, the Great Depression hit six months after Mom settled into her newfound world of rural Iowan farm life, and it would shake America to its economic core. When Wall Street collapsed in October 1929, it didn't affect the De Visser farm immediately. They were still able to sell their dairy products, including cream, and they continued to have economic freedom while the city dwellers in the East Coast were suffering under an almost 20 percent rate of unemployment. Sometime in there, Dad's parents died. No fanfare or detailed remembrances from family members living then. That was it. Garrett died one month after Maatje.

Despite being pregnant most of the time, Mom seemed happy and enjoyed her new life. After Dad's parents died, Mom and Dad began to shine. There exists one photograph of Mom and Dad "dressed to the nines." Mom wore a fashionable flapper dress with a matching French cloche, a headcover with white trim and a dashing blue daisy—a "feel goodery" as they say, and definitely not one to be worn to a Dutch Reformed Church, where modesty and somberness reigned. Mom styled! Dad wore a pressed suit and pants and snazzy fedora, which he always cocked to the side, and a gold pocket watch and chain hung relaxed from his front suit pocket.

I studied that photograph and wished I could have known my parents then, especially Mom, when she was a carefree spirit, full of life and making up for lost time—not in a debauched manner, but by living, just living. All the preachers and priests who may rail against fun things, even in moderation, to heck with them. She may have even had a nip of brandy from time to time.

Dad played saxophone in a local jazz band. He'd sling the saxophone over his back, hop on his Indian, and boot-scoot to Rock Valley, a larger town, to play gigs on many weekends. Mom attended some of his gigs and maybe even danced.

Late one evening, Dad was driving home on his Indian, lost control, and crashed into a drainage ditch. He crashed into loose gravel or sand, sending him apples over apple cart into the deep ditch. He flew over the handlebars headfirst, landing in a neighbor's cow pasture, barely missing being decapitated by the barbed wire fence he had seen at the last minute. The Indian motorcycle ended up in the deep ditch this side of the fence. Unhurt, Dad regrouped, crawled back through the barbed wire, awkwardly pulled the Indian back out onto the road, and checked for any observable damages. Finding the Indian surprisingly undamaged—just dirt clods under the frame and fenders—Dad cranked it to life and drove home, none the worse for wear. When he later told Mom that he lost control, the drinking part may have been left out, giving Mom a sanitized version to pass down to me.

I never got to witness Mom or Dad in that carefree lifestyle: motorcycles, jazz band, stylish clothes. Maybe the motorcycle incident curtailed their adventurous outlook because when Mom found out that Dad almost smeared himself out on a country road on that damn motorbike, she made him sell the Indian. Shortly after, Dad stopped playing in the jazz band, and both of their lives became less colorful.

Life became vanilla.

7

BLACK SUNDAY

We sail within a vast sphere,
ever drifting into uncertainty, drifting end to end.

Blaise Pascal

I n the 1920s, Iowa's farm population was of two minds regarding rural living. On one hand, farm families were real-izing the effects of social deprivations in rural living. Town folks were outdistancing the farm folks regarding modern conveniences and social opportunities. On the other hand, farm families wanted to live much as their parents and grandparents before them, comfortable with certain social deprivations and loving the farm life.

Children of farm families generally received inferior education in the rural schools and did not or would not have the opportunity to attend higher grammar schools. Likewise, most farm families did not have electrical lights, central heating, indoor plumbing, or electrical appliances. But farm families did use the newest invention, the automobile. Dad had the shiny green Chevy Coach, the latest model. Not your ordinary Iowan farmer.

Then the drought of 1934 hit. It is recorded as the worst drought to hit the United States in a thousand years. Scientists from NASA and Lamont-Doherty Earth Observatory looked at tree rings dating from AD 1000 to 2005. They documented exceptional severe-drought events, determining that the bone-dry drought of 1934 was off the charts. The worst drought had occurred in 1580. Seemingly, the southern states east of the Mississippi River and a spackling of northeastern coastal regions were spared.

Nineteen thirty-four came in with a climatological bang. Dust storms etched the flat landscape with black dirt blizzards, carrying Iowa's topsoil to states east of her and destroying the crops. Fourteen dust storms hit Iowa in 1932, increasing to twenty-eight in 1933 and portending a horrific year ahead. By May 1934, over a period of two days, high-level winds lifted 350 million tons of topsoil, carrying it all the way to the Eastern Seaboard. Even ships, some three hundred miles offshore, saw dust collecting on their steel decks.

At first, resistant to giving up, my family hunkered down through the 1934 devastation and prepared to restart their farming in the spring of 1935. Mom sold her flock of sheep, wool and all, and together with the $3,000 she'd saved prior to her marriage, got enough cash to secure a loan from Citizens Savings Bank of Lester, Iowa. They had good credit and had regularly paid about $50 a month for the other farm loan, which was almost paid off. With the purchase of more dairy cattle, Mom and Dad somehow survived that year and continued to pay off their farm mortgage as they tried to restart their farm business.

Dad handled money well and resisted federal aid because "we aren't socialists depending upon government." Mom agreed and added that receiving federal aid amounted to idolatry. My parents' opinion on organizational aid, while common for the Dutch, was not popular. The Dutch were victims of social bullying due to their refusal to join unions and trade organizations. In Grand Rapids, Michigan, Dutch homes, churches, and schools were burned down because of the Dutch workers refusal to participate. The Dutch believed the Lord would provide and bless them if they labored.

For those who accepted it, federal help came January 15, 1935, with FDR's Drought Relief Service, which was a cattle buyback program. It was a lifeline for the rural families in the Midwest. The federal government paid $14–20 per cattle head. The cattle unfit for consumption (about 50 percent) were destroyed. The remaining cattle were processed by the federal government in food distribution to families nationwide. Begrudgingly, farmers gave up their herds, which helped many to avoid bankruptcy. My folks gave into secular influence and accepted US relief money. The temptation was too great. The government paid a better price than the local market could for meat and milk.

The unabated heat and drought also brought some of the worst foes for farmers—insects! Grasshoppers descended in black clouds on the farms, a scourge my parents considered second only to the drought. There was anecdotal evidence of grasshoppers eating the wooden handles of plows, hand tools, shovels, rakes, and pitchforks. Similarly, cinch bugs rode in on the drought and hot weather. Largely unhampered in their migrations, they pursued their customary seasonal life cycle in the Corn Belt, infesting first the wheat and small grains and then the corn. They spread over territory far to the north of their usual range, owing to a succession of hot, dry summers. They were rated as "bad" well up into central Iowa. Farmers in the northern Midwestern states entirely abandoned fields of considerable size.

The Dust Bowl continued to blow through April 14, 1935, which would come to be known as Black Sunday. Black Sunday caused extensive damage, knocking hopeful farmers back on their collective heels. Cash crops died before they even poked out of the topsoil that was left from 1934. An additional 850 million tons of topsoil were blown off the southern plains during

1935 alone. Following Black Sunday, President FDR enforced new farm regulations. The implementation of crop rotation, grass seeding, and new plowing methods began to have a positive impact, reducing dust storms by 65 percent. But only the change in the high-pressure system over the western coast of the US stopped the drought completely, bringing relief by the fall of 1939. But these regulations were too late for many Midwestern farmers, including my family.

By August of 1936, when the second worst drought hit the Iowa Plains, my family gave up. My oldest sister/aunt witnessed Dad at the kitchen table, in tears, with his forehead on his folded arms. She had never seen him emotional before. She would never see him in that emotional state again. At that point, she said, Dad's spirit died.

Sometime between the winter of 1936–1937, the De Vissers gave up.

8

A FROSTY RECEPTION

A good neighbor is a fellow who smiles at you over a back fence but doesn't climb over it.

Arthur Baer

When a cousin informed Mom and Dad that there were jobs available in Fremont, Michigan, they packed up as many belongings as they could fit in the now-aging Chevy Coach, along with six children under the age of eight, and set off for western Michigan. They hillbillied eight hundred miles to Fremont in the dead of winter. The weather must've held up because there were no horror stories of mechanical trouble along the way.

Resettlement in Fremont came without an initial hitch. The family rented a small farmhouse and a couple of acres on Gibson Avenue, just north of town. Nineteen thirty-seven seemed rosy as they unpacked the luggage-laden green Chevy Coach.

It was an unexpected opportune time for the family, thanks to Dan Gerber, Sr. and Gerber Baby Foods Company expanding operations from strained vegetables for toddlers to baby cereal and formula. Dad got hired at Gerber as a boiler man, then later worked in the warehouse. He was now in full employment.

Mom and Dad saw nothing but good things in front of them. Finally, a respite and some job security. The children, giddy with new surroundings, marveled at the trees. It was the first time they had seen trees. The trees brought some comfort to Mom because she missed the Dutch elms from Sheboygan. Henry would attest that the next seventeen years were the best times of his life. Yet for Mom, not so much.

Their closest neighbor was a widower, an Englishman named Mr. Frost. They shared a driveway with a raspberry patch delineating a border in flux. There was no fencing. The raspberry patch was so close to the edge of the driveway that by summer, the growth just about touched the passenger side of Dad's motorcar. Mr. Frost had retired from Gerber years before. He was expecting a quiet solitude of boredom as he slow-motioned into a future of aging. Sitting on the stoop of his white farmhouse, he quietly anticipated nothing specific in his new monotonous existence as he watched his new neighbors pull up noisily, unpack, and offload a mass of unregulated children. He cursed his luck. It could have been a nice couple with no kids, or maybe a spinster teacher just hired for the growing Fremont High School.

Luck bedeviled . . . and loud children at that.

It wouldn't be long before the swirling laughter and incessant energetic chatter ground into his brain. The children couldn't stay on their side of the shared driveway. And the mother sometimes disappeared for a day or two. It seemed the eldest girl, the tall one, would be taking care of her siblings—and the mother inside, doing what? The husband, who was much older, would, at the break of day, shuffle to the Chevy Coach and head off to work, coming home at dark. Those kids ran around like wild Indians, a dervish of activity, carrying on with no awareness to property lines.

Frost muttered as he sat on his stoop, watching the children. He didn't like them near his car. Newer than theirs.

His missus would have probably told him to relax. The kids weren't hurting nothing. "They're just kids, hon." He could hear her voice. But her voice faded from his mind, now that she was gone, and it frustrated him to not hear her clearly anymore. Another side effect of aging: facing a monotonous, useless world alone.

The children's busyness worm-wiggled into his brain.

The long school year helped him regain some peace and tranquility. The parents, when around, didn't bother him. They spoke a broken English. He knew from their accents they were Dutch. Fremont had become the northernmost Dutch enclave in Michigan. Hardworking folks . . . kept to themselves.

Frost liked his privacy. Isolation growing day by day, he enjoyed falling into a routine of purposelessness and coffee, sitting on his stoop, watching time slide by. He was adapting well.

Then school was out. The children's clatter stoked up early and continued until dark. Two of the kids, a boy and a girl, were the troublesome ones. They were running around his raspberry patch and his nice motorcar. It wasn't cheap, and it was his only connection to his old buddies from Gerber. He would drive into town and sit out at The Old State Bank on Main Street and gather with retiree friends and watch the townsfolk go about daily business. Eventually, the social interaction and talking about the Gerber days diminished, and he elected to stay home and work hard at doing nothing but wash his car and tend to his garden.

Unfortunately, his raspberry patch was close to the driveway, and that's where he had always put it. Before the new family arrived, the garden was fine. Why should he change? Just keep those damnable kids under control. Discipline is what they needed.

The missus's quiet voice in his head did not rise to the level where he could take her under serious consideration. "Just ignore them . . . take up another hobby.

And you should not have that garden so close to their property." He had repeatedly gone out all summer. Now that it was August, neighborly gestures disappeared, and the storm of social angst was brewing.

It was a Saturday when all hell broke loose on Gibson Avenue.

Had his wife, Martha, been alive, what was about to happen would not have happened.

Mom was in the kitchen and heard a ruckus outside in the driveway. It sounded much different from the happy, nonsensical chatter, different from the general calamitous goings on of children. She heard the kids screaming. What she didn't hear was Dad, who had been outside working on the yard. She heard another male voice in English. It was crazy Frost!

Mom mustered her energies away from washing the breakfast dishes and moved quickly toward the caterwauling. She reached the porch step in time to see hoe-wielding Mr. Frost attacking Dad.

The children scattered in four directions as if a bomb were about to blow.

Mr. Frost raised the hoe overhead and swung hard downward, striking Dad across the shoulder with a handle-to-bone *crack*!

Dad warded off the next blow by backing away and not engaging his attacker.

Years later, removed from the incident, none of the witnesses could explain Dad's passiveness. He was a powerful man, yet he didn't fight back as Frost struck the hoe onto Dad's shoulder again. As Old Man Frost redoubled his attacks on Dad, Dad remained eerily passive, almost martyrlike, waiting for the blows.

Mom, now outside, leaped off the porch steps and boot-scooted toward the two men. Like a mother grizzly, she attacked the attacker, so much bigger than her, but her counterattack caught Frost off guard. Mom slapped the side of his head.

Before his attention could focus on the fiery wrath of Mom, he felt a kick to his shin. Then another and another. He backed off, retreating to his side of the driveway. He dropped the hoe.

Mom, now fully armed with Frost's hoe, sidearmed it in his direction, striking him below the waist. Mr. Frost buckled and fell back, retreating into his house.

That should have been the end of it. A domestic dispute gone a bit overboard was not that unusual in those times. But that wasn't where it ended. This dustup between neighbors settled Mom's sense of justice, but Mr. Frost apparently thought otherwise because after the tussle, the police arrived.

Frost's account came as gospel. Mom would have to go to court and defend herself and her children.

9

JUDGE HOWARD

Learn to do right; seek justice. Defend the oppressed.
Take up your cause of the fatherless; plead the case of the widow.

Isaiah 1:17 (NIV)

Mom found herself in district court. She was subpoenaed for an evidentiary hearing before Judge Howard at the district court in White Cloud, Michigan, along with two of her children, Nellie and Gordon. Piecemeal recollections created an opaque retelling of the judicial proceedings. Mom's action against Mr. Frost was deemed defensible and she was not charged. Nellie and Gordon were alleged to have continued on a path of delinquency, destroying a portion of the raspberry patch that lined the driveway between the De Vissers and Frost.

Mom pled her case in front of Judge Howard, who sat on his throne in his black robe, acting as if a god, as she put it. Mom defended her kids, who were preteens, claiming they were "*kleine kinderen*," poor little ones. Mom pled the case that her children were good children and did no unruly acts toward Mr. Frost's property, nor could any histories of delinquency be proven. Yet there were stories about Nellie that were troubling.

According to a story told by her sister Mae, Nellie once had a "dustup" with a dog. As the story went, Nellie may have been bitten by the dog, but in the end, Nellie killed the dog. She killed it with a Coke bottle.

A few years before the court case, as a teenager, Nellie actually tried to kill Gordon. It happened while Dad was haying. Nellie, Gordon, and Janet helped load hay into the back of a pickup. For reasons unexplained, Nellie snuck into the cab and behind the wheel. Dad and Janet were in the field, carrying hay back to the truck. Gordon remained standing in the back of the pickup, ready to receive and stack the hay bales.

Nellie suddenly put the truck in reverse, and then quickly revved forward. Gordon, who had been unsecured, flew out of the truck onto the ground. Nellie looked back through the rear window, and seeing Gordon off the back, quickly put the truck into reverse to run him over. Gordan rolled out of the way, the left rear tire clipping him. He came up, swearing. Nellie laughed. Dad pulled Nellie roughly out of the truck and slapped her behind, then sent her crying back to the house.

Gordon, on the other hand, was just a raucous teenager, beginning to smoke cigarettes, sneak beer, and get into schoolyard scuffles. Gordon did not exhibit Nellie's anti-social behaviors but got caught up in Nellie's sociopathic escapades.

In any event, Mom found herself in front of Judge Howard with little defense. Timing is everything. And as timing would have it, Frost's children had grown up and moved away. Frost was in no mood to accept gaiety and children's spontaneity into his life, let alone onto his property or near his new car. Mom, on the other hand, came from a deeply rich Dutch culture going back some four hundred years, where children were allowed childish freedom so as not to burden their fragile nature with heavy adult-world things. She stood at the ready to protect her children from sober adult oppressions.

The two points of view collided.

Without photographs, the only "evidence" was Mr. Frost's assertions. Judge Howard ruled in favor of Mr. Frost, handing down a court order sending Nellie and Gordon to reform school for a specified time, with no visitation. When the verdict was read, it set Mom off. She berated and cussed at the judge. She was fined for contempt of court, which she never paid. Nellie and Gordon were taken away and put in reform school for a time, to return a year or two later.

Reform school may have been good for Gordon, since when he came of age, he eventually enlisted into the army, became a marksman and sharpshooter, and served with honor during the Berlin crisis. He matured and helped the family, sending most of his army paychecks back to the family during their financially lean years.

While Gordon seemed to benefit from reform school, Nellie continued her wayward path, unchanged. When I knew her, Nellie exhibited a passive aggressive persona, mercilessly abusing her fraternal twin, Janet. She would verbally taunt Janet for her cognitive failings, making Janet angry and setting her off into tirades. Nellie smiled once Janet blew up. It was Nellie's sport.

Nellie eventually married Johnny from Grant, Michigan. He was a Catholic, to Mom's dismay, and worse, an alcoholic and abuser. Johnny died at the age of forty from acute alcoholism but produced five children. Johnny's and Nellie's youngest son joined the US Army, and while home on furlough, he was killed in a single vehicular accident. Their son had been driving drunk and crashed into a tree at over a hundred miles an hour. When the police arrived, they noted a bumper sticker on the crashed vehicle that read DAMM. It stood for Drunks Against Mad Mothers. The Michigan State Police used photos of the destroyed vehicle as an educational poster for high school students thereafter.

Nellie lived the rest of her life single and eventually passed away in 2017 from dementia.

As a child I frequently heard about Judge Howard, all in the negative. Mom's paradigm became my paradigm. The courts were against the De Vissers. Right or wrong, I began to distrust the judicial system. I would take this misguided perception into my teen years and early adult life, all to my detriment.

When I was fifteen, this distrust was reinforced when Mae's husband, Corwin Green, was put on trial for arson. I attended the jury trial every day, seated prominently in the front row behind the defense counsel table. I witnessed the proceedings unfold. It looked bad for Corwin, who was alleged to have set his house on fire.

The first fire had started when Corwin and Mae were out of state visiting friends in Illinois—a solid alibi. The fire inspector could not definitively conclude in his report that the first fire was deliberately set, but when the second fire started, Corwin was in town. They had him. The allegation was that Corwin had started a second fire to gain more insurance money. Corwin stated he had an alibi for both fires. He did have an alibi for both, but I knew he was guilty.

What the prosecutor could not prove, and what I knew, was that Corwin drove back to Michigan under the cover of night and set the first fire. The police could not nail him for the first fire, but the second fire was going to be Corwin's undoing, so they thought. Corwin had the motive and opportunity because he was in town for the second fire.

I sat in court and knew the truth.

Corwin did not set the second fire.

I did!

After the first fire, Corwin had propositioned me with a tempting offer. He agreed to teach me how to drive his stick shift Rambler, which would help me pass driver's training, if I set fire to his mostly burned-down house. So, one night in February 1968, Corwin took me driving the backroads and somehow, perchance, ended up in front of his burned-out house. He produced a flashlight and matches, instructing me to jump out of the now slow-moving car.

"There is a five gallon can of gasoline and rolled newspapers in the back bedroom under some burned debris," he said. "Go in the house and reset the house from that bedroom. Spread the gasoline around and back away. Then set the rolled newspapers on fire and throw them. Stay back. The gasoline will do its work."

I jumped out of the rolling Rambler and watched Corwin drive out of view. I was in utter darkness, but for my small flashlight. I found my way through the heavy snow and into the back bedroom. I did as instructed, and the back bedroom went up in a wide, wild flame. I ran out and waited for Corwin's return.

Corwin came back into view, and witnessing the flames, claimed I did a fine job. The second fire reduced the house to rubble, undistinguishable as a dwelling at all. *I did do a fine job*, I thought.

During the trial, I thought the cops would interview me, for obvious reasons. But I was never interviewed, and I thought about this conundrum during the entire trial. Here a man was on trial for something he didn't do (well, conspiracy, yes, but that was not the charge) and not on trial for the crime he did commit. And there was the actual arsonist—me—sitting in the courtroom in the front row, watching Uncle Corwin take the fall. He did not turn on me but sat stoically at the defense table. Certain prison was in his immediate future.

Then came the verdict.

Not guilty.

Not guilty! How could that be? They had him dead to rights.

Then the reason behind the verdict came forth. The defense attorney had successfully argued that since the first fire had destroyed all the gas and electrical utilities and the utility companies had shut off the utilities before the second fire, according to the State Fire Code, the second fire could not fall under the definition of arson. There could be no arson because Corwin's home was no longer considered a viable home or structure. It was more akin to a rubbish pile or a burning pile of wood. Under that definition, there was no arson, and Corwin was being tried for something that did not occur. A fire, yes, but arson, no.

And there it was: a crime committed by two people on separate occasions, but no one went to jail. I did learn to drive a stick shift out of all of this. A silver lining for me.

And the family, knowing most of the whole ignoble drama, did not berate or punish me— another silver lining for me. What was sinful or not right was seemingly getting overlooked.

10

GRACE OR FATE

If we believe in a logical, loving, and purposeful God, we trust that suffering will have meaning in a world in which we are only short-time visitors.

Maribeth Vander Weele, from Joy of Job

From 1938 until the spring of 1944, the family settled in. Old Man Frost died. Judge Howard retired. Things quieted.

By 1944, Mom sported two sets of fraternal twins: Lillian and Lorraine, and Janet and Nellie. She had Mae, the eldest, and two boys: Henry Jr. and Gordon (the only child to be born in the hospital). She was tired, her body giving out now after all those living children and five stillborn births (including another two sets of twins that didn't make past day one). She had also developed acute diabetes along with her epilepsy.

Henry Jr., now eleven, was the spittin' image of Dad—blond, blue-eyed, chiseled facial features, handsome, and healthy. Then, one day in March coming home from school, he complained of severe back pain. Henry Jr. wasn't a complainer, not even when he shut his finger in a door once. He just said "oh, shucks," shaking his hand in the air as if that would heal it and going about his kid business. Sometime earlier, he had been pushed down a flight of stairs at school by bullies, but he did not complain of that, either.

Yet this pain was different. He cried when the back pain increased. Dr. Geerlings, the family doctor, was called, and he quickly made a house visit with a large black medical bag in tow, chock full of diagnosis tools, needles, and pills. Dr. Geerlings had just started his practice in our town and remained Mom's favorite physician, mainly for his humorous bedside manner and, probably more so, for his being a member of our church.

The doctor checked Henry Jr. for vitals and joked with the boy. Did he have any girlfriends, careful of getting cooties, favorite subject in school? Then his demeanor changed when he noticed Henry Jr.'s blood pressure was elevated, something not normal for a backache. He palpated Junior's kidney area and found it tender to the touch and swollen. Dr. Geerlings had Junior urinate. The urine was bubbly, a sign of too much protein called albumin. That showed kidney issues. Severe kidney issues. Without trying to alarm Mom and

Dad, Dr. Geerlings said Henry Jr. had to be hospitalized immediately for more tests. Just a precaution.

In the hospital, Henry Jr.'s condition deteriorated. Dr. Geerlings called in medical experts from Grand Rapids. Henry Jr. was diagnosed with Bright's disease, incurable back then. He was treated with warm baths and dietary restrictions eliminating red meat and cheese, but that was about all modern medicine in 1944 could do. His condition worsened, and on one visit, he claimed to Mom that he couldn't see. Soon after, he hemorrhaged, became unconscious, and fell into a coma. He died a day later.

Mom often told me of Henry Jr.'s death. What she emphasized was the lead up to his death, which she told to the nth degree, and often. Anytime when there was peace in the house—a rarity in the human condition overall, but in our house exceedingly rare—she would bring up Henry's death. They pushed him down a flight of stairs at school was her mantra. That's what killed him.

Her daughters, especially Mae, the family gossip historian, claimed something entirely different: He died of a kidney failure. And actually, she was closer to the truth since Bright's disease was a kidney disease; she just didn't identify it as such.

What seeped into my consciousness as a child, and even into my preteens, wasn't the causational thing in Henry Jr. dying, but that he died. He was only eleven.

I was eight or nine when I started doing a morbid countdown to when I would reach eleven. Every year with a new birthday, I foresaw my possible impending demise too. Would I die before or at eleven as Henry Jr. had? I sincerely believed I would die.

Kids will create their own odd realities. That is the way kids' minds work, unable to process reality due to a lack of good information, reassurance, and a brick ton of life experiences.

It didn't help when during generic unconnected conversations around the dinner table Mom randomly threw out, "The old must die, and the young may die," with the emphasis on "young." Or, "You, young man, by the grace of God, are alive."

Those mantras were just the added ingredients that sent me into a melancholic paradigm of a Death Watch. My death. I could die just like Henry Jr. Added to that was the unwelcoming weekly chore my parents gave me as a child: accompanying them to the Maple Grove Cemetery to visit Henry Jr.'s grave. They conscripted me into watering the plants around the headstone and the large raspberry ceramic planter, as they stood quietly staring at his tombstone.

Throw in all those morbid variables, and you have a tortuous new headspace for this kid they adopted. Were they saying, Watch out—you will or could be next? Or did they simply have me help with watering his grave? Whatever their motives, I tortured myself, generally at bedtime, that I quite possibly would die the next day, or probably the upcoming week.

The only relief was my twelfth birthday. Then and only then did I let go of the fear of dying . . . I had made it past year eleven. Whew! By the grace of God, I survived. Or was it just fate? I was the lucky one, undeservedly the lucky one. Did my life have more meaning than Henry Jr.'s? Why did God have nothing in store for Henry to do in God's kingdom, except maybe to be fodder for bullies and lingering sadness for his parents?

Yet for Mom and Dad, 1944 had more in store for them. And for them, grace wasn't setting foot in their household anytime soon. Something more horrifying would visit.

11

FEAR IS THE POLIO OF THE SOUL

Fear is the polio of the soul which prevents our walking by faith.

Clarence Jordan

As Allied soldiers prepared to storm the beaches of Normandy, a boy in western rural North Carolina took sick with a fever and a stiffening neck. Hickory, North Carolina, was to witness devastation laid upon its most innocent and vulnerable—its children.

Other communities would soon follow suit, with children getting fevers, stiff necks, then becoming paralyzed. America was about to repeat a deadly viral epidemic, last seen in 1916 when the United States experienced its first polio epidemic, initially in New York City. Surrounding communities closed their doors to non-residents, relying on heavily armed policeman to patrol the roads and rail stations, searching out fleeing New Yorkers with their children. By October 1916, 27,000 lives were lost; 80 percent were children under five years of age.

This second polio epidemic, which would not be controlled until 1955 with the release of the polio vaccine, was about to touch our family. In August 1944, just six months after Henry Jr.'s death, Mae took sick with a fever and a stiffening neck.

A virus seems to hold keys and search out a host. Once its key fits into a human genome, it attaches and reproduces, taking over the host in a battle of survival. The polio virus got Mae. Mae was fourteen, a vibrant and seemingly healthy young adolescent, taking care of her younger siblings, helping around the house, prepping the kids for church and school, then herself setting out to school on foot. And yes, through sunshine, rain, blizzards.

One afternoon after chores, Mae went to her usual piano lessons. She had to walk approximately a mile. Mae felt a slight discomfort in the back of her neck. A stiffening. But she focused on her piano lessons with Mrs. Van den Zee. Halfway through the lesson, she said she didn't feel well and complained her neck hurt, more than stiffness. Mrs. Van den Zee excused her with the usual Dutch *harrumph* and let Mae walk home.

When Mae told Mom of her neck pain, Mom

excused her from making dinner or washing the dishes. Her sisters could pick up the slack. Mom directed Mae to lie down and rest. She'd be fine.

But Mae wouldn't be fine. By dinnertime, she had a fever, then by late evening, she complained her legs began to get "feely." By morning, "I can't move my legs!" Her limbs wouldn't function. Sometime later, when she tried to sit up and do homework, her thumbs refused to work. She couldn't sign her name.

Mae's condition worsened; a fever came and went, sometimes spiking to 104 degrees. Mom knew exactly what was happening. It was late August and still hot. That meant one thing. Infantile paralysis. Polio! A parent's worst nightmare. Every summer since the beginning of the twentieth century, the virulent polio virus attacked children, especially those under the age of five, an annual scourge.

But Mae was a teen. Surely, Mae couldn't have polio.

Yet Mom knew that President FDR had contracted polio in his adult years. Medical experts in the early twentieth century believed the virus randomly destroyed muscles. What the health experts knew was that they didn't really know. But in their hubris, they had to do something. They gathered data (as in our COVID-19 and H1N1 pandemics) and attempted to make some semblance of medical sense out of this destroying virus. Person-to-person contraction was believed to be the catalyst. We must disinfect everything!

When Mae couldn't get out of bed. Mom sat with her, applying cold neck compresses and massaging her limbs. Helplessly, Mom could only watch with growing dread as Mae began to complain she was having difficulty breathing.

By the following day, at sunrise, Mae was gasping for air. Mom called Dad; they had to act. Mae had to go to the hospital. Mom knew the local Gerber Memorial Hospital couldn't help; it was good for minor illnesses and broken bones, not for an invisible enemy like a virus. They had to go to the big city, Grand Rapids Butterworth Hospital. Mom and Dad set out with Mae lying in the back seat, her breaths rapid and weak.

As far as Mom could see, Mae was dying.

Mom had heard polio was spread via person to person, and there was no option in that small farmhouse for any kind of social distancing. Six kids, all under fourteen, snuggled in a bedroom the size of a back storeroom, in only two beds. She later attested to the horrid thought that all her kids would catch the virus, for they all had been in direct contact with Mae. Yet none of Mae's siblings contracted Mae's polio virus! And all their lives, they were never vaccinated.

Mae was the only person to contract polio in Fremont in 1944. And that fact did not escape Mom. She inventoried the ghoulish circumstances affecting her kids and began writing poems to God, in simplistic style.

According to her nephew, Stephen Vander Weele, who was a professor of English at Calvin College, her poems were full of deep emotions. A tribute to her faith, like Jacob in the Bible, who wrestled with the Angel until daylight, Aunt Agnes was going to wrestle with God to receive a reasonable answer. Where was God's grace for her family? What sin had she perpetuated to receive this disaster?

Professor Stephen gave me some of her poems after her passing. I was astounded at the direction the poems took. She added a pinch of sarcasm, softly questioning God's future plans for her family. Or was her family in His plans at all? Mom danced around blasphemy, but in reading her poems, I could feel her losing hope in all things. She was at wits end on how to proceed happily and joyfully.

Mae was hospitalized, encapsulated in a new machine called an iron lung. In layman's terms, the machine was a mechanical ventilator to help her breathe. Years later, when I was an adult, she would share stories of those days confined in the iron lung. There was an entire room at the hospital that had victims like her, many younger than her. There was a boy about her age, maybe younger, and they developed a friendship. Each iron lung held mirrors set up over the patients' heads so they could see themselves, and when tilted by the nurses, the patient could see their fellow patients to the direct left and right.

One morning, Mae woke up and greeted her young friend. There came no response. A nurse informed her that the boy had passed away in the night. Mae said, "That was the way it was." The virus could continue to progress upward until the involuntary muscles like one's lungs stopped functioning. "The iron lung saved those who couldn't breathe, but there was yet no machine to assist the heart pumping when the virus destroyed it. My friend didn't have a chance."

During those months living vicariously through a machine, she told me she had lots of time to talk to God. In the darkness, in that sterile hospital setting with the grinding and growling of many iron lungs, she met God. She prayed to live. She prayed and prayed and talked to God.

"I accepted His will that if I had to die, He would give me the strength to handle death," she told me.

After six months encased in the metal contraption, doctors informed Mom and Dad that they were turning off the iron lung. When Mae was notified, she desperately petitioned against it, as any frightened child would. The doctors told her it was time. Could she breathe on her own? A nurse was directed to unplug the machine. Her eyes widened in horror as the nurse pulled the electrical cord. The growling mechanical engine stopped. She could feel the machine release her and stop massaging her lungs.

Mae gasped. She said at that point, she accepted death.

She inhaled. Suddenly, fresh air filled her lungs . . . fresh air! She tried to breathe deeply but couldn't.

Mom and Dad stood at her bedside and watched helplessly as she kept trying to breathe. They were small breaths, her lungs weak from lack of involuntary activity, but her lungs were working. She could breathe independently.

She recounted that her prayers were answered and her faith reassured, despite remaining a paraplegic. For the rest of her life, Mae would be wheelchair-bound and would need twenty-four-hour care. Even in this diminished physical outcome, she would be thankful. Mae's faith was strengthened, and the rest of her life, she would retell the story of living in that iron lung and then getting her life back. She believed that God spared her. Mae told her testimony of faith to anyone who visited her. All friends and visitors came away feeling humbled and equally blessed being in Mae's presence. Mae went on to live a long life filled with gratefulness.

Meanwhile, Mom wrote more poems to God.

DOWN MEMORY LANE
By Agnes De Visser, circa 1945
(unedited)

It was just two years ago
That Mae was stricken with polio—
A severe headache
And pain in her back—
Though we did not think it a polio attack.

The doctor came and shook his head;
He went away and came in the noon
With the health doctor.
They decided to take her to the hospital.
Reverend Schuring was then called. . . and prayed with her
That if it could be God's will to restore her to health again.
She walked to the car and into Blodgett she came,
There for a few weeks or for a length of time to remain.

She remained quite well for only five days
When slowly on her lungs became paralyzed.
The iron lung was ready in case
Something would happen—and it did,
For she got all blue in her face.
Her life had almost faded away
So all the doctors and nurses quickly put her
In the iron lung.

There she remained for six weeks,
Four months before God took away her brother—
That is surely something for a father and mother.

September 1 Reverend Schuring came and said,
"Mae is very low . . ."
That was surely again a heavy blow.
Her mother replied and said,
"Must all my children be carried to the grave?"
He answered, "Just be humble and brave."
So we all three went.
And a day in the hospital was spent.

Rev. Schuring said,
"Here we are again at the same old place."
That gave us all a disturbing face.
So we could see her off and on for a minute or two,
For she wasn't allowed to talk but one word or two.
We went home and gave her into
the protecting hand of God,
For He alone for us could help afford.

She started improving, and soon five minutes each day
Out of the lung she could stay.
Each day a little longer: first a half hour,
A whole hour, then a half day.
A whole day at last, and then came discharge day.

Now Sister Kenny's hot pack treatment, day by day
For six months long, every single day,
For all her muscle power was gone.
The iron lung saved her life,
but plenty things were still wrong.

Seven months in the hospital she spent,
And with Easter, to the Blodgett Home she went.
She didn't like it in the Home at all.
Too lonesome she was for the doctors and nurses—
Especially Montgomery, her top favorite nurse.
That friend watched her very close so
she would not get worse.

12

THE HAPPIEST PERSON IN THE WORLD

It is not how much we have, but how much we enjoy,
that makes happiness.

Charles Spurgeon

Mae survived polio but did not fully recover. The polio virus left her wheelchair-bound for the rest of her life. Her involuntary organs and muscles were spared, so she could breathe on her own. Her voluntary muscles, such as legs and torso, no longer functioned. She had to be helped in and out of bed, had to be positioned in her wheelchair by her sisters almost hourly. If she had an itch, she needed someone to scratch it. She needed care in every way, and her dignity, too, was taken from her as others had to aid her in dressing, bathing, and bodily functions.

Lorraine was working as an apprentice nurse's aide at Butterworth Hospital when Mae took ill, so Mom assigned Lorraine to be charge of Mae's care. Lorraine begrudged this for decades, saying she'd had to quit her job as a nurse's aide and come back home to help Mae. Every day, Lorraine would get Mae out of bed, dress her, comb her hair, brush her teeth, apply general makeup, powder her face, and push her into the kitchen for breakfast and coffee. Lorraine had her own problems, developing the same acute type of epilepsy as Mom. Maybe it was the medication to quell Lorraine's grand mal seizures that made her become a mercurial person in her own right.

Anyone approaching Mae would be confronted by a beautiful woman with bright hazel eyes, shiny black hair, high cheek bones, and a full, beautiful smile, all encased in a faulty body with no ability to move. Only her neck and her facial muscles could she control. Her legs were unable to move anymore. Her arms atrophied.

But it was her hands that struck most as shocking. Mae's hands atrophied too, and the tendons in both hands curled her fingers inward into the palms of her hands. It displayed an intense deformity and the definite outward sign of what had ravaged her when she was child. She could not straighten them. I tried. As an innocent kid, I tried to open those fingers, and they wouldn't move. They were permanently bent inward. She said she could not remember when they were straight.

Mom said it happened once Mae came out of the iron lung. She went in with straight fingers and came out crippled—legs, torso, and those fingers. She had feeling throughout, not like a quadriplegic or paraplegic involved in a horrific car accident, gun incident, or diving accident, which would permanently destroy their nerve endings.

When I was two years old, Mae graduated with the high school class of 1955, after being held back a year. A male classmate had made her a table in woodshop class that dovetailed onto her wheelchair as a desk. One thing Mae could still do was write. She just needed help getting the pen fitted into her crippled hand. Get a pen into the fingers of her right hand, and she could push her body and her elbow back and forth with the pen securely affixed between the bent fingers. Remarkably, she wrote in cursive. More remarkable, she wrote with exquisite handwriting. She used a real ink pen, too, one with ink cartridges. Her cursive was so exquisite that she quite possibly could have petitioned to make it a font in today's world of computer fonts. She could have called it Mae Font.

There are photos of me, as early as two years old, sitting on her wheelchair table, assisting her, setting her pen in her fingers. She would instruct me gently and patiently. And soon, I was helping with other fine-motor tasks such as replacing old empty ink cartridges with new ink cartridges. Mae had a paperweight to hold down the paper as she wrote letters, and I would move the paperweight when the page was filled. The unlined pages were filled with deep blue ink of astonishingly cursive renderings.

She would write approximately fifty letters a week, each letter single spaced, double sided, and at least several pages long. The pages were beautiful. She was beautiful.

Her spirit filled me up with warm feelings. I came to be a needed helper. As a child, I was small enough to sit on her desk as she wrote. Or I could stand on the foot pedals of her wheelchair and hand her a drink of water or soda pop, cookies, or part of a sandwich. I felt good being near her.

It's been said, happiness is a choice, while liberty and freedom are a value. Liberty and freedom can be attained through the right geopolitical circumstances, although history has shown that to be a fluid rarity. However, being happy is a direct choice, a direct action. Happiness begins as an action within oneself.

Horrific and outside situations may attempt to wrestle that control away, but the determinate factor shaping our state of being is within our control. Circumstances—such as receiving life-threatening diseases, loss of friends and family due to unexpected deaths, accidents, crippling injuries—will wobble our efforts to be happy. The bombardment of horrific news from mainstream media constantly impinges upon our happiness. In the end, we are the sole determinants on being happy. Our destiny begins with us.

I saw that in Mae.

After Mae contracted polio, she could have become bitter. Her mood could have turned black, yet her spirit remained intact. Mae exhibited a warm expression about her countenance. I cannot recall a day she exhibited a bitter outlook. The irony is that my family determined somewhere along the way that they collectively were going to be unhappy. Mae's positive attitude did not rub off. My family chose a different demonstrative tack. They chose bitterness with a strong influx of victimization.

I watched this transpire throughout my childhood. As I helped Mae, I adopted her attitude despite the dominate prevailing winds of familial unhappiness. It was as if by being physically close to her, I received distinct recompenses of joy and wellbeing. When Lorraine rained verbal and physical abuses upon me as a child, I seemed to weather those tumultuous episodes because of Mae's influence. Mae had given me a template by which to live.

Mae lived with polio from the summer of 1944, then fourteen years old, until her death at seventy-six. Mae rarely exhibited a sad exterior. She confessed to me that at night she would speak quietly to God. Sometimes anger, sometimes sadness came through as she talked to the Lord about her plight, but she said she would never during the light of day exhibit any sadness or gloomy impressions. She saw it her mission and her love of God to be a joyous and happy person.

13

FAMILY AND RELIGION

*Family quarrels are bitter things. They don't go according to any rules.
They're not like aches or wounds, they're more like splits in the
skin that won't heal because there's not enough material.*

F. Scott Fitzgerald

The children were now adults in their twenties and thirties, but still like unregulated teens. Dad began drinking, and Mom became mercurial.

Mom stopped writing poems to God and stepped away from a personal relationship with God and, in that vacuum, replaced it with religiousness and odd pious rules. She became less spiritual and more religious, which directly affected me. She refused me the same freedoms as she had allowed her biological children. When she applied these religious tenets to me, biblical righteousness and grace became orphans, and her rigid thinking became more black and white. Her daughters, too, seemed to adopt this new pattern, especially Lorraine. Dad didn't care one way or the other and allowed the women to rule over me.

And into this developing maelstrom, I was born.

The entire family forbade me to watch TV on Sunday, claiming it was sinful. What we did six days a week should not be done on the Sabbath—an implied theology in our Dutch Reformed traditions. But Mom and the girls began to slip and watched TV on Sunday nights. I was about three or four when I recall this change occurring. I thought this new shift in dogma applied to me too.

It didn't.

Walt Disney's foray into the weekly television show, *Walt Disney Presents* (1958–1961) and later *Walt Disney's Wonderful World of Color* (1961–1969), came on Sunday nights at 7:30 p.m. One Sunday night, the family TV was turned on to the channel showing the introduction of *Walt Disney Presents*. I excitedly sat down to watch with the entire family. One of the adults (probably Lorraine) said I could not watch TV and I had to go to bed. I remember crying as I watched the Disney introduction, fireworks exploding behind a beautiful fairytale castle (a replica of Neuschwanstein Castle, a world-famous European tourist attraction). I watched the TV screen as a female cartoon fairy swooped into view with a magical wand, producing brilliant swashes of colors in front of the castle.

And that is all I saw.

Lorraine or Mom said, "To bed."

I protested and pleaded, but Lorraine rough handled me up the stairs and to my room. To this day, I have never seen one Disney TV show. It hurt beyond articulation that as a little child, I sat on my bedroom floor, listening to my family watch a show that I, too, wanted to watch. Their actions were another abandonment of sorts.

Church life was accelerated in my conscripted participation as I reached reading age. I was forced to go to church twice on Sunday, along with attending Catechism class in fall and winter. Memorizing the Heidelberg Catechism was a daunting mental dive into deep theological abstractions and Christian exegesis. I attended Sunday School, and for added measure, Young People's Choir. I was not allowed to play outdoors on Sundays, only sanctioned to read religious books or do homework.

Weekly restrictions included, but were not limited to, no attending school social events (wherein there may be the peril of dancing), no card playing, no gambling of any kind, and no theater movie going, for all were sins according to Reformed theology. When I was in college, I read The Stone Lectures, a seminar given at Princeton University in 1913 (or so), by Abraham Kuyper (then

President of the Netherlands), who expounded on the rationale of the abovementioned religious restrictions. His arguments were reasoned, yet not so much my family's. For them, restrictions became rigid and legalistic, going beyond good Christian parenting.

As a kid, I began to suspect those restrictions set upon me were fluid in Mom's house because I knew from listening to my sister's sordid teen tales that they committed violations of all those restrictions, absent of any moderation. I saw the hypocrisy, but until I became a teen, I was resigned to my fate to follow the burgeoning religious beliefs thrust upon me.

Mom began punishing me for odd things. Generally, when children do inappropriate things like slugging someone in the face, or lying, or stealing, a child will grow up learning right from wrong. Not so in my family. My family, especially a few of Mom's daughters, lied regularly, frolicked with boys, and violently and psychosocially abused me. There were no punishments for that. And in that environment, I did not learn good from evil, but I learned that anything my family felt was wrong—like speaking out of turn, speaking up at all, not eating adult-sized portions of food at meals— would fashion punishment, such as sitting for hours at the dinner table. Placing any object on top of the family Bible, which was rarely read out loud, would receive intense belittlement and a hit across the back of the head by Mom. Yet when I started stealing (even from

Mom), or fighting in school, or exhibiting poor social skills in the classroom, or showing high absenteeism, or receiving incredibly low grades in school, there were no repercussions.

Mom developed a reputation as an angry woman at best and a crazy person at worst. Not too crazy, just enough to ostracize herself. She had no friends. One cousin would, on occasion, visit from Grand Rapids, but that, too, stopped after Mom threw a bowl of soup at her cousin's spouse. Apparently, the spouse had made disparaging remarks about Mom's kids, or the manner in which she raised the darlings, and from across a large dining room table came a full bowl of soup.

Churchgoing added no solace for Mom. When the family attended church, we ended up in the farthest pew in the back, just enough room for the family. Intentional? I never gave it much thought when I was a kid.

Mom may have known her social standing in our church community as subordinate and chosen to sit in the last pew on the west side. Maybe from her history of epileptic seizures she knew the back pew was the best positioning in case a tonic-conic seizure hit her. The dread of knowing she could have a seizure in church must have been so disquieting. Had I had epilepsy, I may not have gone to church at all, or least I might have sat in the basement and listened to the sermon over the intercom.

Church members knew of Mom's temper, and her pew positioning made other congregants fill up the front rows first, which must have delighted the Dutch pastors. For the slothful, they would catch themselves sitting close to Mom, saddled with an unpredictable woman. Her burgeoning reputation as an off-centered, hotheaded old woman with odd outbursts that had nothing to do with rights or wrongs, did not abate. She probably thought she was justified, a perfect show of self-righteousness; indignation was what was precisely and necessarily needed. She began to justify striking out at inanimate objects—all things great or small, alive or inanimate. This comely old woman in a frumpy, flowered dress, would cuss out an uneven elevation in a city sidewalk or an unruly church door.

On one occasion, as church was letting out, a congregant in front of her forgot to hold open the door for the parishioners behind. The doors of the church were heavy swinging doors, heavy oak with no device to close slowly. One of the doors swung into Mom's face, striking her squarely across the right side of her face. Upon impact, Mom launched into a most violent manner of cursing (to this day, my peers recall and remind me at school reunions). Mom struck at the door with double-fisted fury while cursing in two languages, Dutch and English, and, to boot, in a dialect not often heard in our town: Zeeuws (a Dutch/Flemish dialect, called Low Dutch by Dad). Mom knew all three "f" words, and she fully educated the exiting parishioners around her of that acquired insight.

I was directly behind her when the oak door smacked her head. (I was probably fourteen years old then.) Swearing in church! What an added shame that poured over me. Adding to my horror, directly behind me was my school crush, Nancy, and her dad, who was an elder in the church and pillar of the community. I couldn't look at Nancy, but I knew she was behind me.

I did not go to school that upcoming week, feigning illness.

It was difficult to hate Mom, even back then. Mom did her best as she, in a binary mental state, attempted to hold herself together when the prescribed holy silence was mandated once the church bells rang. Generally, she was good in church. Pious and reverent. Yet she was disintegrating. Every little thing produced internal angst. Her state of mind had fused dream state and reality . . . the commingling a disquieting mental struggle for the remainder of her life. Unregulated doses of Phenobarbital and horrific doses of Dilantin didn't help.

Physicians in the 1960s guinea-pigged people with epilepsy using cocktails of newly regulated drugs. These medical experts were guessing, which resulted in their patients losing their actual minds. Adding to that, Mom suffered from a deteriorating pancreatic system. Her doctors were just getting a grip on diabetes with insulin. Yet changing dosages based on blood tests that were only taken once monthly tended to send Mom's blood levels completely out of whack. She would suffer frequent incidences of insulin reaction and an occasional life-threatening diabetic coma. I witnessed three diabetic comas and innumerable insulin reactions.

Mom didn't seem to have relief from anything, within or without.

She had to do housework along with Janet, while the other daughters were going out day and night, consorting with male teenage sinners—men on motorcycles, carnival bums, and discreet church boys who later would become pillars of the community, elders, and deacons in the church.

But Mom tried to remain steadfast in her Christian faith as best she could. She had set some spiritual standards for our household. We remained orthodox in Reformed theology. She made certain I was going to church every Sunday. I learned the Christian hymns. Somehow, despite our lower socioeconomic status, she and Dad sent me to a privileged and private Dutch Christian school with high academic standards. She set moral standards as best she could and hoped the church community and Christian schoolteachers would shore up this boy born out of wedlock.

Mom was tired, but every time epilepsy or diabetes or her kids knocked her down, she would gather the broken pieces of her mind and put them back together best she could and fight again to make things right and true. It would be up to the family to follow the ways of the Lord, the faith of our fathers, to be true until death. And she did it alone while Dad spun into a world dimly lit, taking his daughters with him.

Though Mom's brewing resentments garnered anger toward mostly religious folks, especially the Catholics, Baptists, and rich Christians (Christians having fun and having too many indulgences in modern society), Mom still believed in being in God's service, but she didn't know what that service entailed.

14

TWO KINDS OF MEN

*There are two kinds of men: the righteous who think they are sinners,
and the sinners who think they are righteous.*

Blaise Pascal

I adored Dad. Mom not so much. I prayed for Dad. I did not pray for Mom.

By the time I was born, Dad was nearing retirement from Gerber and the girls were entering their late teen years. Dad stopped attending church regularly. He seemed cool and acted cool in a stoic mannerism. Very rarely did he show emotion of any kind. He was an old man, sixty-five, when they took me in. I remember saying my prayers, including prayers for Dad to remain healthy.

Mom was not the kind of person a kid could pray for, in my mind's eye. As a kid with undeveloped discernment skills, I viewed Mom as the villain because she was cranky and seemed mean. Little did I know that what was occurring behind the scenes would prove my hero a villain and Mom, the antagonist, my eventual heroine.

Dad never said a harsh word or reprimanded me for anything done wrong. He was old, yet powerfully strong, as I was to witness when I was ten. He once took a son-in-law and pile-drove him into the living room carpet after the man foolishly besmirched one of his daughters. Dad was then eighty, and his son-in-law thirty-five, a farmer in his own right.

One Sunday, the entire family visited a family friend, Henry Ippel, a farmer living north of town. Dad took me into the barn with Henry to slaughter a hog. Henry Ippel bordered the hog into the barn and Dad wrangled the 650-pound creature, slicing its throat. A death dance ensued, Dad avoiding the three-inch razor-sharp tusks while holding a butcher's knife, the same knife he had chased me with after downing a fifth of Four Roses whiskey when I was five years old. The hog squealed and swung his head, trying to slice up Dad. Dad slit the throat, oxygen-rich blood gushing six feet or more across the cement barn floor. Dad easily backed away as the dying beast charged him, sidestepping the hog's every move until the creature dropped. A last twitch, feet kicking out, then still.

Dad was strong . . . dangerous. But he was Dad.

My unwavering hero worship vanished one sunny summer day. I was ten, eleven, or maybe twelve years old. I went upstairs to my bedroom, possibly to get some toys or a book, when I heard odd noises in the adjacent bedroom, just beyond the landing at the top of the stairs. My bedroom had no door, was open, and encompassed the landing of the stairs. I reached the landing and heard a giggle. It was Janet. Then my eyes caught Dad and Janet together in Janet's bedroom. They were in an embrace, Dad doing most of embracing. Dad saw me and shot a soulless glare, his eyes darker than I had ever seen before.

Somehow, I knew I'd better scoot back downstairs, which I did, skipping every other step. I exited the house, found my friends, and we played. I forgot what happened. The mind of a child translates horrific events differently than adults. I had limited experiences, which made me unable to put things in good order. It was a visual puzzle with many key pieces missing. I never reported the incident and never spoke of it to anyone, not even to my buddies. Even now, this is a difficult thing to share since I loved Dad more than Mom.

Now as an adult and a trained professional investigator, I understand Mom's daughters' erratic behaviors as they reached teenage years. Dad broke the boundaries between parent and children, and he set off dynamics which had horrid repercussions in our family. The daughters began acting out, absorbedly promiscuous with relish. They documented their escapades in diaries, sneaking out of church to romp with ill-disciplined boys and older men! The girls stayed out late, going to movies and dances, ignoring curfews, and sometimes simply not coming home until the following morning. Two daughters, fraternal twins, Lorraine and Lillian, shared a friend, Roy Thomas.

According to Mae, Roy Thomas came to town one spring day and Lorraine and Lilian became enamored. Roy coaxed a Harley Davidson down Main Street, straddling lanky legs across a chrome-polished motorbike, exuding an aura of a big city, bad boy adventurer. He wore tight blue jeans and a black leather jacket, open to exhibit a bare chest and emblazoned with a motorcycle gang logo embroidered in black-and-white lettering on the back—a large scorpion in the middle of the bikers' patch. It read: Scorpions-Detroit.

Roy hired in at Gerber; he purchased a mobile trailer, set it up at a lake just outside city limits, and went to work.

The sixteen-year-old twins would find themselves in his embrace, often staying the night. He was twenty-nine.

Sisters Mae and Nellie would find their own adventures from church choir boys. Sunday church brought many a young man to Mae's assistance; it took four men to lift her wheelchair up some twenty steps and into the sanctuary. I always admired the men for being so kind and willing. It wasn't easy lifting her up while wearing Sunday best and black dress shoes with smooth soles in winter conditions. I thought these guys were true heroes. In time, I learned these men were being given certain favors from her between Sundays, with sisters Nellie and Lorraine giving covering fire so the parents would be none the wiser.

Dad tried to reign in his daughters with little success. If the Janet incident was any indication, Dad no longer held moral authority.

Mom became more upset as the family deteriorated into unwholesomeness and circuitous chaos. With no extended family close by, and no friends, Mom fought this alone. And maybe that is why she did what she did for Janet.

Mom secured a job for Janet as a housekeeper with a family down the street, away from the shadowy influences venting inside our home. Janet was twenty-one in 1952 when she took the job with a pious Free Methodist family, the Scotts. Being regulated to domestic duties at home during her teen years gave her some semblance of worth, as her sisters pranced about town. Janet was a great housekeeper and especially enjoyed washing dishes and sweeping.

Initially, Janet enjoyed the housekeeping duties; this family was nice and patient, as Janet, cognitively impaired, had to be retrained daily on some duties. The job gave Janet something to brag about. She was earning money, and even though most of the money was going to the family budget, which Mom controlled, she was contributing and felt valuable.

But as good intentions often go in different directions than planned, and so did the housekeeping inkling. Sometime during her housekeeping job at the pious Free Methodist family's home, Janet wound up pregnant. It could have been Dad, but Janet claimed it was a sixteen-year-old boy named Bob Scott at the house she was cleaning. Janet professed to her dying day that Bob impregnated her—but she was wrong. Maybe the teen did take advantage of her. Bob's older brother, Chester, confessed to me that Bob was not of good character, and he certainly believed Bob got Janet pregnant.

The truth, confirmed many years later through DNA results, was that Bob did not get Janet pregnant. An Arthur Chester Salisbury did.

Arthur Chester Salisbury would often visit the Scotts' home because he liked to see his grandchildren, Bob and Chester. As a grandfather, he was in his sixties in 1952 when he impregnated Janet!

Obviously, in time, Mom discovered Janet was pregnant. Mom didn't know what recompense she might have but to wait until the third trimester. Then, Mom and Dad secretly shuttled Janet to Grand Rapids, some sixty miles away, to give birth to the baby in Salvation Army's Booth Memorial Hospital for unwed mothers.

I was that baby.

And for the family, I came unwanted and uninvited.

15

DIVISION STREET

A man who carries a cat by the tail
Learns he can learn no other way.

Mark Twain

When I was born, the family had moved from their small farm west of town and into town, onto Division Street, just inside the city limits.

My Dutch maternal grandparents became Mom and Dad (though they didn't legally adopt me until 1966), and my biological mom, Janet, and her siblings, my biological aunts and uncle, became my sisters and brother. The day I came home from the hospital, I joined a family of two aging grandparents (now my parents), five aunts, one of which became bad-tempered and a mercurial bane to my existence, and one wayward uncle, who cared little for my existence.

Black-and-white family photos showed a happy demeanor with these adults, me smiling and being a cute and curious addition, like a pet puppy. The family doctor confirmed that I was a bright and healthy child despite my genetic predispositions, within standard limits of being normal.

"His eyes are bright," Doc Geerlings said.

I was a cute toddler, endearing from photographs. God shaped my nose agreeably, but not as a prominent Dutch nose—not a nose wide as the signature of the Van der Weeles nor proudly prominent as the De Vissers. An agreeably defined Welsh nose fit my face nicely. Aryan features—blond hair and blue eyes—escaped me, for I came out with thick black hair and brown eyes, olive-toned skin, and thick black hair with a defined "widow's peak." This would stand out when I later went to a Dutch Christian school, my peers being blond, blue-eyed, and white-skinned. In time, my ears grew a tad bigger for my head, and the left ear protruded out a bit more than the right ear, which became my only gripe to the Lord in His sculpturing of me. I would be teased in school for these visual malformities, which would give way to bullying and subtle ostracization. I would not understand this as I maneuvered through Christian private schooling except to feel the attacks, believing this to be a normal rite of passage.

Mom named me and not Janet. Janet wanted to name me Edward. I didn't look like an Edward or an Eddie. Mom named me Sherwood Allen—Allen because she too believed I was the product of the sixteen-year-old Robert "Bob" Allen Scott. I believe it was her shot at the Scotts that she knew about what they wouldn't confess to or apologize for.

My arrival caused Dad to continue to work at Gerber an extra five years. A possible first demerit to my value—Dad working beyond sixty-five. My family members repeated this fact to me throughout my childhood, and I took it as he cared enough to work longer because he saw me as a valuable member of the family. But I was mistaken, and in time, my family's true motives would be brought to light.

Our Division Street house was a drab gray slate exterior with a sizable yard, where Mom planted raspberries and tiger irises. Dad watered the plants on summer evenings and then snuck off downtown.

Janet lost her job as a housekeeper and started running away from home. In 1955, she came up pregnant again. It was a boy. The father was unknown, but unlike my destiny, this second baby was delivered to an adoption agency in Muskegon and placed for adoption. The new family doctor, Dr. Masters, told Mom he could help. He sterilized Janet. It was a blessing for both Janet and Mom, but illegal as hell.

By the time I was two years old, my sisters were

entering the boy-crazy teen world, and with that, I became an afterthought the majority of the time. Things were uneventful if I was good—that being a quiet, a compliant lad. But I was a normal child with normal needs, and this became an impediment to the girls' social lives, and with that perception, patience for me would be the rarest of commodities.

I would find out the hard way.

There were incidences that, upon serious self-examination as an adult, I now question whether or not they were attempting to do me harm, like the time I fell down a flight of stairs. When I was three, maybe four, I recall standing at the top of the stairs on the second floor, then bumping down thirteen steps to the first-floor opening. I always thought I just fell. But what was a little boy doing at the top of the stairs alone? I don't remember crawling up those stairs. I could have been alone because, if memory serves, I was not watched well enough in general.

Did I slip, trip, or was I pushed? There is nothing there but the memory of being at the top of the stairs, then falling, ending mostly frightened but unharmed at the bottom of the wooden stair step. I cried.

No one picked me up.

One of my most vivid recollections, from which I have never fully recovered, occurred when I was two years old. The event burned into my psyche and deeply affected my outer, inner, and spiritual journeys to this day.

I distinctly recall standing in our living room by a large plate-glass window that bordered an adjacent enclosed porch and crying. With arms extended, I attempted to communicate to my family members something that I felt was unfair. Was I being just an irritating little child at that time? Did I feel a frustration from unfairness? Either way, I distinctly recall the helplessness in getting my message across to the wide-eyed audience.

They were at the dining table having a late breakfast when Lorraine rushed in upon me. She crudely picked me up by my prominent left ear, pain spiking into my brain, then tucked me into her hip, my head fully exposed to her free hand slapping me in the face. Treating me like an irksome house pet that had just messed on the floor, Lorraine carried me out of the living room, beating on my head and face as she storm-marched through the kitchen and out the door into an adjacent enclosed washroom.

My head grazed a washing machine as she clawed at me, her long witch-fingers digging into my side. We reached the far end of the enclosed porch, me trying to wiggle free when I saw my upcoming fate.

Lorraine was taking me to the cellar!

I screamed, "I'll be good! I'll be good!"

She cursed at me as we descended the concrete steps to the bottom of the stairs. The air temperature became colder, as the moldy-stale smell of the basement filled my nose. We reached a wooden door. With one arm,

Lorraine unhooked a stout door and unceremoniously deposited me onto the cellar's cement floor.

I launched back up, pleading to her that I would be good.

With cold eyes, Lorraine pushed me backward and closed the door.

I heard the lock latch. "I'll be good . . . I'll be good. No . . . no . . . noooo!"

I was trapped and could not find the light switch.

I was left in mostly blackness, a small coal-chute window on the far side of the cellar giving off diminishing light. Lorraine's footsteps stomped overhead as I screamed. The screams gave way to helpless crying, then weakened to soft blubbering. At some point, only whimpering came forth from my chest.

I scurried over as close as I could to the coal-chute window but could not reach it to open it. I found a fruit crate and tried to stand on it and reach the window latch. I fell. At that point, I realized there could be bugs, or worse, spiders about. I set the crate back up and sat on it with my feet off the ground, knees to my chest. Spiders could be anywhere. Everywhere!

As my eyes adjusted to the darkness, I fumbled again to the window and again climbed onto a wooden crate. I felt the latch and tried to open it. The latch was nailed shut! I was trapped.

As I continue to whimper, I was now afraid of more than spiders, my imagination conjuring up creepy crawling things that surely were in the room and soon to be under my feet. I returned to my protective sitting position and listened.

Overhead I heard my family walking and talking, as if I didn't exist.

I felt abandoned.

That feeling of knowing my family allowed me to be rough handled into a basement without coming to my aid is unsettling to me. Even my biological mom did not come to my aid. I think she may have screamed too.

I continued to hear them talking, occasional footsteps moving from living room to kitchen and back and forth, as if nothing were abnormal about a child imprisoned in a Michigan basement.

The light from the coal-chute window seemed to taunted me. Through that window I could see grass and sky, a beckoning, sunny day. I called out to God, hoping His angels would come and rescue me. No angels came. I was left to my own devices until the adults above my head saw fit to come get me.

Decades later, as I was retelling the event to a childhood friend, Dave, he abruptly stopped me midsentence. "It was not a basement or a cellar," he said. "You were imprisoned in a crawl space."

Now a professional investigator, I decided to revisit the scene to corroborate my memories. I led Dave back to that Division Street house. We asked the current occupants if we could view that basement. We knew this was an odd ask, but we were greeted kindly and allowed inside. We walked through the living room, and I noted it was much smaller than I remembered. The kitchen, too, was tiny, with little room for one adult to turn from the stove to kitchen sink.

Dave and I walked through the enclosed porch and approached the cellar stairs. It was tight and musty smelling, colder as we reached the base of the cellar door. I unhooked the same latch and opened the door. To my shock, I had to duck under the doorframe as it was only three feet high. One step down and I entered a room that could only be described as a crawl space, housing a small natural gas furnace and a small shelving unit we had used to store canned goods. The room was a six by eight feet large. The small window was only two feet off the ground and tapered downward, making it difficult to climb out of if one were a child.

The only missing piece was my age at that time. I needed empirical evidence as to my exact age. I took height measurements of the coal-chute window, and then I examined the height of my children. As is common with parents, I measured my children's growth by marking their height on an interior door frame. To my surprise, my hypothesis as to my exact age was correct. When Lorraine threw me in that cellar, I was two years old! Maybe two and a half.

On that day, and other days like that, Lorraine continued that sort of punishment for an unknowable amount of time. I cannot recall how long I was confined or how frequent was this punishment. Nothing in my childhood would reach that level of hopelessness and terror.

The experience taught me that neither God nor His angels would come. It was the beginning of when my prayers were not going to be answered. Maybe my prayers even then were no good. It left me feeling horrifically vulnerable, for I was on my own with no help coming. Later, I had the same feeling when bullies cornered me in kindergarten, beating me, tearing my clothes, choking me, and slugging me in the stomach— that there was no hope of heroes. I learned I had to just ride it out.

That cellar experience taught me "it is what it is," and "you're on your own."

When I was left to my own devices (which was most of the time, except Sundays), life became lively.

On one such occasion, I was allowed to watch TV. My favorite cartoon was *Popeye the Sailor*. I saw him eat spinach from a can and become super strong. One day, we had cooked spinach. My folks were surprised when I suffered down a large helping of that slimy green substance. I ate the spinach with gusto, knowing I was going to be like Popeye.

After dinner, I went outside to play. A kid idea struck me. I approached an old-growth maple tree in our front yard and gave it a good ole Popeye haymaker, smacking my little fist into the tree. The impact hurt.

What was I thinking?

I never ate spinach again.

On another occasion, when I was about four years old, I found myself in a neighbor's yard playing (adults term it trespassing), throwing a ball on the roof of an old farm implement shed on the far end of the property line. The yard held enormous walnut trees and the property was owned by two elderly twin sisters in their eighties. As the story went, the sisters, for whatever circumstances, never married and simply resigned themselves to living together. They were so sweet to me and accepted my playing in and around those majestic walnut trees. I made a game of throwing a red rubber ball on the shed's roof, where it disappeared momentarily, then try to catch the ball as it came bouncing back down toward earth. I played for hours on their property, content in my loneliness.

One morning, while playing catch, I saw a large fox squirrel in the trees. *Let's see if I can catch that squirrel,* I thought. I dropped my ball and glove and watched the squirrel's movements. I studied the squirrel's gesticulations and saw a pattern develop. He circled counter clockwise, stopped, nose in the air, and then downward circled the tree again. When I first spotted him, or her, the squirrel was high in the tree, but he seemed to be after fallen walnuts. *If I sneak up on him, I can catch him by the tail.* I had heard Dad claim that to catch an animal, the best way was to put salt on his tail.

At age four, what that really meant escaped me, but the key, I thought, was grabbing the critter by the tail. He didn't climb straight up and down but circled the base of the tree and up into the branches. I cozied up to the tree, the squirrel unsuspecting, and waited at the base of the tree for the squirrel to wind his way back down. Sure enough, its beady-eyed head peeked around the tree.

I saw my chance and grabbed its tail. I had a wild rodent by its tail, and at the other end was a mightily displeased furry fella, and before I could formulate an effective plan for what to do with it, the squirrel curled upward and bit me. It chomped on my right index finger. I succumbed to its toothy entreaty, cried out in pain, and shook the squirrel free, letting it fly back up the tree. Blood squirted from my finger.

I went home a learned naturalist and probably got my injured finger bandaged. I never told the adults how I bloodied my finger, and as I recall, they didn't ask. Just another child scratch.

I was lucky. I never got rabies. And I became wiser. Carrying any creature by the tail—experiences such as this one can best learn no other way.

16

THE BIGGEST HOUSE ON THE BLOCK

Mental health: having enough safe places in your mind
for your thoughts to settle.

Alain de Botton

By the time I was ready for kindergarten, we had moved from the cramped Division Street house to Maple Street, a spacious house just south of Main Street, with a neighborhood filled with large families and many kids my age. With so many kids, we would field two baseball teams for our summer sandlot games. Other summer evenings, we played frozen tag and hide-and-seek, approximately twenty-five kids running and laughing in a predetermined neighbor's yard. When the streetlights came on at the corner of Merchant and Maple, that was the understood signal to go home.

I thought I lived an eternity on that street, although it was only six years. But it was my golden age. And despite the family's down drifting into mental illness and growing violence, those years on Maple Street were without childhood equal. Intense highs and lows in my kid world, with adventures and mishaps—I breathed it all in fully. School would be a mixed bag, but school for any kid roller-coastered between drama and dreams. My fondest memories were on the outside, under sunny summer days, or under the streetlights of Maple Street. Everything was grand.

Twenty-two Maple Street was the biggest house on the block, a two story with two full baths, an enclosed sun porch, a stately living room with a natural gas fireplace (which my parents never used), and five bedrooms. Included in the real estate sale was a refurbished barn that was made into two rental units. It would be a welcome income stream for my parents. Curiously, Dad did not attempt to fill the two rental units. Only by happenstance, a divorcée, a single mother of one boy child, elected to live in the bottom floor all the years I lived there, but the upper floor unit remained empty. Dad still owned the Division Street house. He never filled that house either, letting it remain empty until the time we moved back into that dingy dwelling.

A nice-sized yard set between the two dwellings. The rear of the house held an elevated porch, which provided quiet solitude away from us noisy kids. A linear raspberry patch butted up to our property line and the west side of our new neighbors' garage.

We had the best residence on the block, by far. How and why we got into that house never became clear. As a kid, I did not concern myself with such matters. All I know is my best memories came out of that move because I had kids my age to play with and space to roam.

Yet my family didn't share in my delighted outlook. Twenty-two Maple Street also became a lair of childhood horrors with roller-coaster escapades. The girls became more aggravated and increasingly violent. Their collective temperaments inflamed with outbursts, which shocked the neighbors and showered shame on me, especially at school.

The girls were now in their early twenties. Lillian and Nellie had married, but Lorraine and Janet remained at home. Inside and outside worlds parted. Inside the "four walls," as Mom called our domicile, my world became nuts, an intensifying influx of violent outbursts by Lorraine and Janet and Mom devolving into mental illness. I began to experience night terrors. It would be where Lorraine went full banshee, exacting violence on me and Janet. Janet, in turn, began to run away from home frequently.

My friends were forbidden to come over and play, not in the yard and not in the house. I have no explanation for that. We had a new beginning, a nice house, and some social stressors gone with two daughters off and married, with grandchildren in the offing. We were living in the golden years of an economic boom, low taxes, a car in every garage, and full-time employment. A glorious time to live in America, and especially in Fremont. As my inside world was nutty, the world outside was generally heavenly.

Possibly, Mom hadn't fully recovered from the past. And she would never recover. She tried, especially when we went on vacations. But a darkness seemed to hover over her. As a child, I heard her often repeat the lament of the loss of Henry Jr., and Mae getting polio. No child had died of Bright's disease but her Henry. No one else in Fremont had contracted polio but Mae. These unresolved hurts, along with personal spiritual issues, ate at her.

Mom became jealous of others prospering but couldn't see that we also were in a good economic place. The positive possibilities were all around us on Maple Street. Yet she could not see that brightening world laid out for her. I do believe the Lord had heard her prayers, and Maple Street would, at times, be a long-term respite for her, a place of peace.

She turned a bitter eye toward her church and fellow congregants. She muttered often as to why other church members prospered while her family suffered so. The prospering church folks she knew shouldn't be prospering. They were sinners too. Why did they deserve easy street while her road was filled with ruts and stones? Were they that better than her? They were not honoring God, or at least in the manner Mom perceived; they should be reverent. Yes, they went to church, but their hearts were not right. Many times, she saw them cheat their neighbors in business deals or cheat employees if a business owner—unethical profits in her mind, a wicked lifestyle.

I heard her and her daughters talk about the sins of prominent church members. They spoke openly, naming members in the church secretly having wife-swapping parties. Why did they prosper while living wickedly? Their children were healthy. Why didn't their kids die or succumb to life-altering diseases? They were wicked, but their wealth increased. Did God not see? They did not even have ordinary troubles, and they were not plagued as she. They were prideful and wore bright-colored clothes and drove shiny motorcars to show off that pride. There was no humility in them. They were shameless and carefree. Perhaps Mom thought dark imaginings ruled them. Maybe she believed she tried to be pure of heart, and for what purpose—more and more suffering for her children?

While I was growing up in that household, envy wormed inside of her soul and grew exponentially. She became jealous. She reached the crossroad of envy; her spirit became poisoned as she crossed over and became resentful. She would take everyone down with her. Once she crossed over, all she could see and think about were the folks above her and how well-off they were, despite being more sinful than her.

I recall her spurning one church member who had purchased a motorcycle. "Look, there goes Harold, full of pride, and riding that motorcycle on Sunday."

Our town prospered under the protective economic umbrella of Gerber Baby Food Company, which at this time controlled 78 percent of the baby food market, giving Fremont full employment. Everyone seemed to prosper. Money was flush in the community and our church, making up 33 percent of the town's population, prospered mightily.

The Dutch farmers surrounding Fremont had invested in Dan Gerber Sr.'s company at its inception. In the 1920s, Dan Gerber, Sr. had petitioned and promised that if the Dutch farmers of Fremont bought Gerber stock in lieu of monies for their cash crops of peas, green beans, wheat, oats, apples, cherries, peaches, and blueberries, they would do well in the long run. The farmers put trust in his company, and by the 1960s, the Gerber stock had flourished, making farmers rich. Our town was the second richest city in the world per capita, second only to Kuwait City, Michigan. In a town with a population of only 3,200, we had a hundred families who were millionaires!

Our church, flush with Christian charity, graciously paid my full tuition to attend the coveted Fremont Christian School, a highly academic private school. We were poor but of Dutch ancestry, which gave us a step up over Norma and Alex, who lived in the purple house closest to our church. Yet our family acted poorer than we really were. The three sisters, still living at home in their thirties, received Social Security disability benefits. Mom and Dad were now retired and receiving Social Security checks, too, including one for me, or because of me.

We had three rental properties. We had one longtime renter, but the other two rentals remained unoccupied, and Dad never seemed engaged enough after retiring from Gerber's to advertise those units. Dad and the three daughters could have easily run a lucrative rental business. But they didn't. They complained about their lot in life and enviously besmirched "rich" townsfolk for their ravenous appetites for nice things.

We were not that poor. We were middle class. Yet Mom and Dad made it as if it wasn't so. We ate poorly . . . a daily diet of potatoes and yellow wax beans or peas made up our supper. I choked this protein-less dietary regimen down for years. I learned not to talk back or whine, but to act as if everything were fine. Starches made up my diet at a time when I needed protein. I was allotted milk for breakfast only. For lunch and supper, I was restricted from drinks of any kind. They never gave me an answer to that oddity. The adults had coffee at every meal, sometimes tea. I had nothing to get those tasteless meals down my gullet.

There were days I would wake up shaking, my whole body trembling from lack of protein. I would rush downstairs and eat a half box of Kellogg's Frosted Flakes, or a half loaf of bread with peanut butter, and only stop when the shaking disappeared. When playing outdoors, I would go to the Mendham's house and wait around for lunch and eat there . . . my first meat protein experience: hotdogs! To this day, I am addicted to hotdogs—with casings or without, Kosher or unkosher.

I now had a way by which to escape my house and enter another that provided me with meat protein. For me, the world was brightening. For Mom, the world remained a constant tortuous thing, dimly lit, because the neighbor kids were getting into her raspberries.

17

KINDERGARTEN

God made the Idiot for practice,
and then He made the School Board.

Mark Twain

I soon discovered that school was going to be no different than home life, just a brick ton more structure.

On the first day of school, I stepped off the morning bus and was met with a punch to the stomach. I bent over and vomited my hard-earned breakfast of Frosted Flakes. I looked up and met my welcoming committee of one, a kid my size snickering. He did not hit me again but ran laughing into the school building. I managed to get to my school room but a bit off-centered.

The perpetrator was Dick W., whose father was a

pillar in the community. Their family attended a Dutch Christian Reformed Church in the same small town. Our town built churches on almost every corner, with the majority being Dutch Christian Reformed, Reformed or Calvinistic, Presbyterians, or Congregationalists. The Baptists and Methodists were also well represented with several churches. Mom did not like Methodists, and not until I was older, much older, did I understand her point of view. Gerber Executives were encouraged to attend the Congregational Church, probably because it was Calvinistic light. It was primarily for show, said Mom. One of my bullies from the Congregational Church during my preteen years was the reverend's kid.

I recovered from the belly punch as Mom's warnings flooded into me. "We De Vissers are always being bullied. We will always be the brunt of violence by people who have it better." Janet had been bullied too. She was walking home from kindergarten with her sisters when several fellow Christian schoolgirls began teasing, making fun of her severe speech impediment. One of the belligerents swung her tin lunchbox, striking Janet square on the side of her head. Janet cried. Her three sisters did not go to her defense; instead they ran home, leaving her to fend for herself.

Mom somehow got wind of this incident and pulled Janet out of school. Janet didn't return to school until the district began a pilot special-needs system. By then, Janet was fourteen and unable to read. She never caught up.

I suspected school was not going to be any better than home. At least I knew the pulse of the family. I could sense danger often, thereby protecting myself. When Mom or her daughters went raging, I could sense it. Heck, I could smell the resentment brewing in the air. I would still take a beating, but the vital parts, like my ears, eyes, and head would be somewhat protected due to defensive awareness.

At home I could sense the attacks. At school, not so much—at least at first. I couldn't really articulate it as a five-year-old, but I learned "thin-slicing," a term Malcolm Gladwell defined as the ability to find patterns in events based only on "thin slices," or narrow windows, of experience. Judgments based on thin-slicing can be as accurate, or even more so, than judgments based on much more information.

Kindergarten did not improve. By week's end, recess offered up new horrors. Third graders! At morning recess, we had to be inclusive in the playground with the older kids. I found myself and a few others as entertainment fodder. That first week of school, the three Z. brothers found me. Two of the boys were twins and third graders, farm boys and strong already; the other brother, the leader, was a fourth grader. During recess time they would line up me and the other kindergarten kids (except for Dick W.—his dad was a doctor, so they didn't dare) against the school wall, conveniently just out of view from the teachers' lounge.

The Z. brothers would walk back and forth, then all of a sudden, and god-like, pick a victim.. They pressed almost nose to nose on us, the unfortunate victim receiving a spit full of berating. Then, for laughs, they would punch, slap, and steal hats, stepping on them or not giving them back until after recess bell rang. For that entire autumn during morning recess, I was lined up against the same wall, berated, called names, spit on, slugged, pinched, and for good measure, my shirts or jackets ripped. On a really terrible recess, I would be kicked in the groin.

As a kid I wondered why the teachers were not more visible during recess. Why did they include us kindergarteners with the big kids?

As I reached ninth grade, I witnessed teachers simply smoking in the lounge rooms (back then it was permitted), leaving the schoolyard unattended and the younger more vulnerable kids to fend for themselves. I never reported this negligence. I don't know why. One would surmise that Ms. J., my kindergarten teacher, would have noticed that every day, the same few boys would come in after recess bloodied or crying. Never happened. Winter provided me with the only reprieve. Apparently, for whatever reason, during winter we were left alone.

We were not safe inside school, either. We kindergarteners heard the scuttlebutt that any kid caught in the bathroom would have his head flushed in the toilet.

Luckily, our kindergarten room had its own facilities. But once I entered first grade, I never went to the bathroom during or immediately after school. I was terrified of my head being flushed in a toilet. I would hold it until the school was emptied of potential bullies, watching for the sign of the last school bus driving out of view, taking the bullying bastards back to their privileged world.

And that was that. School was just like home, just a bit more structure and a tad more horrifying.

18

BIRTHDAY PARTY

Don't be crabby—it's only a birthday!

Unknown

The first year after moving to Maple Street started out wonderfully. The family gave me a birthday party, and a grand birthday party it was, with all my schoolmates coming to my birthday revelry. I graduated to first grade at the private school, which was made up primarily of second-generation Dutch kids. My peers' parents were primarily businessmen and professionals such as insurance agents, doctors, lawyers, and farmers.

The birthday layout was royal treatment for me. Large picnic tables were laid out in the back yard with decorative tablecloths, balloons adorned the back porch, and a birthday cake bought from the store was the centerpiece. Set before me lay oodles of grand, expensive, and unwrapped birthday presents.

I was the center of attention.

The day went without a hitch. None of my family members acted out in any embarrassing fashion, and from my remembrance, all family members pitched in to make it my most favorite day. There was ice cream and cake and goody gifts and games for my peers. The day was mine. I felt special, more than just another drop in the ocean.

That was August 17, 1960, and it would be my one and only birthday party.

Thereafter my family would not celebrate my birthdays in any standard manner. I would not receive gifts. Likewise, Christmas celebrations would follow the gift-giving deprivation template, an everlasting disappointment. But at the time, I relished my birthday, playing with all the toys and cool stuff my schoolmates had given me.

Sometime after school started, I came home one day from an arduous day of writing, reading, and arithmetic learning, anticipating going to the enclosed sunroom, my safe place, to play with my birthday gifts. I ran into the house, deposited my Dick and Jane and arithmetic workbooks on the kitchen table, and burst into the sunroom.

I looked around, gape-shocked. My little wooden desk was cleaned off. No toys. The wall shelf now lay barebones. My entire sunroom was void of all my new toys, my birthday gifts gone. Catching my attention was an orange object under my wooden play desk. It was one of my birthday presents. I retrieved the orange plastic football, and carrying it under my arm like an NFL running back, I ran to the kitchen to share my findings.

And, like a first grader, I petitioned the adults as to where my toys were. Mom, Dad, Mae, and Lorraine heard my sad story. Everybody did not have an answer. I was fluffed off. Based on past experiences of beatings or confinement in basements, I knew better than to cry, so I went back to the sunroom. Holding tightly to the orange plastic football, I positioned into a corner and cried.

I knew I could be heard, so I cried as quietly as I could, and when the crying was out, I went outside with the orange plastic football and played solitary football in the front yard, hiking the ball to myself, throwing and catching and pretending ghost opponents were tackling me. For the rest of the autumn and until the snow flew, I returned from school, got my orange plastic football, which I hid in different spots, and played football, making up teams and playing out football scenarios until dark.

The family had to have seen that. Though I was not beaten down, a bit of my worth had been taken from me, another coercive effect on my trust with familial adults.

19

DUTCH CHRISTIAN SCHOOL

We all learn by experience,
but some of us have to go to summer school.

Peter De Vries

In my austere opinion, there is only one solution to successfully navigating school life, be it in public, religious, charter, or private schools. True success in navigating school from elementary through high school is how you manage the world of bullying. Academics for students are just a sidebar in this process. Bullying will never go away without draconian measures, in themselves an institutional bullying of sorts, just in governmental form. Bullying is a sad but constant ingredient in all school environments. Home schooling may make it safe in the short term, but eventually home schoolers have to confront bullying once they reach out into the full spectrum of social interactions. It is just an "is."

And bullying will not go away. Well-intentioned parents, teachers, and school administrators cannot effectively stop bullying. Bullying is akin to water: Where water always finds its way, bullying, too, will skirt around every regulation, social construct, rule, and security measure. Security cameras will only record bullying incidents, not stop them. No, tolerance measures will only create a new bully, a bully targeting high-achieving students on a college track, knowing they cannot fight back in self-defense or they will face suspension. Bullying always finds a path.

First grade presented positive potential. First-grade learning remains a foggy bottom to me. I remember Mrs. S., a young, diminutive blond woman, as my teacher. Mrs. J., my kindergarten teacher, had been older and more or less homely in appearance, whereas Mrs. S. had a bright smile and was the most beautiful person I had met in my early six years of life, quite possibly the prettiest woman in the known galaxy. I think I learned to read in first grade, or at least mastered simple sentencing. The Z. brothers no longer tormented me. Possibly, they moved out to public school, as I do not remember them at all after kindergarten.

Mrs. S. moved around the classroom, personally attending to each kid's scholastic needs. Mrs. S. reflected a saintly demeanor and was patient and nice to me, and in her schoolroom, I found a safe place wherein I learned to read and write, due to her kind stewardship and shepherding. First grade moved forward in ordinary fashion.

Second grade rekindled the kid horrors that I experienced in kindergarten, but this time, the bullying came not from peers during schoolyard recess or in bathrooms, but from teachers and an assistant principal. Bullies would come in adult forms.

My second-grade teacher, Ms. Edna, was a callous unmarried woman of middle age. I cannot recall her countenance except that she sported a mean smile and her hair was always pulled up into a tight bun. If I learned anything, it should have been to not talk during class. Ms. Edna had her ways of rectifying chatty habits. And apparently, I was a chatty boy in school. I demanded attention. I didn't realize I needed attention, but Ms. Edna made me a point of interest. I recall one time in class, when I was talking to Penny Bauman, how Ms. Edna taught us proper attention skills.

Penny and I were engaged in some type of imperative kid conversation, unaware of our surroundings, when Ms. Edna stormed from the front of the classroom and descended upon us while I was mid-sentence. Ms. Edna struck Penny on the face with an open hand. Then she slapped me hard on the face. My face reddened. Before we could cry out, she had scotch taped both of our mouths shut. She forced us to the front of the class, and there we sat, mouths taped shut, for the remainder of the class period.

Penny became compliant thereafter, but I, on the other hand, received this lesson several more times. By Christmas, I think I learned my lesson.

Our school, like many schools, created special events or distraction for upcoming holidays. Christmas and Easter we made projects that we could take home to show off to our parents. Valentine's Day was for me the great determiner that my sister Lorraine had been right about my wellbeing and worth. When the opportunity presented itself, she would tell me that I was "dumb, stupid, skinny, and ugly." It was an ongoing mantra that started sometime in my childhood, possibly about the time I began school. The words bore into my brain and wickedly ambled down into my spirit. I was not at the same level as normal kids. It wouldn't let go, and school reinforced that mantra to the point I believed I was a low-echelon student.

Valentine's Day proved Lorraine's hypothesis. For the holiday activity, we were encouraged to buy Valentine cards and candy (the ones with mushy romantic phrases such as "Be My Valentine") and give them to our "special friends." We would be asked to put our heads down on our arms on our desks and keep our eyes closed as each one of us took a turn going around the room distributing our candies and cards to our special friends. When all the students had accomplished the task, we could look up and see how many goodies we were blessed with.

I looked up and saw my desk empty!

Not one Valentine card claiming I was special to someone. Not one piece of candy. I just sat, sad. It was all I could do while classmates celebrated their cards and candies. I was helpless and could not escape. Lorraine was right. I was not like the other kids. I was not right.

Third grade started out fine, moving out of Ms. Edna's class. In third grade, I learned good penmanship and cursive letters. Math was enjoyable, and I easily held my own, scholastically speaking. I would have enjoyed that year except for the music teacher, Mr. Fink. He was an accomplished music teacher, and because of him, I learned the parts of an orchestra and was exposed to beautiful classical music, both from hymns and the secular genre. The thing that terrified me was him forcing us kids to sing. Singing was not my forte. Even at that young age, I knew I could not carry a tune. I was tone deaf.

But Mr. Fink made each of us get up when it was our turn and grab the American flag in the front corner of the classroom and march around the room singing "Onward Christian Soldier." At least that was the song I ended up singing. It was horrifying for me. The waiting. Then the exact moment to be called. Many of my classmates, especially the girls, could sing without instrument accompaniment, and they could sing in tune.

I couldn't sing in a choir. I was terrified and expressed angst all across my face. He had to have seen that wide-eyed dread look about me. But he didn't care because he called my name and made me sing in front of my peers and in a cappella. I was devastated as I carried the American flag and attempted to sing. Nothing resembling song came out. The girls snickered; others simply laughed. Mr. Fink did not hush them. For the remainder of that school year, I began skipping school on the days Mr. Fink came to class.

I never forgave Mr. Fink. When I got to Junior High, I did everything in my power to get kicked out of conscripted school choir. And I succeeded, but with a report card loaded with "Unsatisfactory."

That year, I again received no Valentine cards.

I advanced into fourth grade. Apparently, my absences, which were quite a few, did not hold me back. Mrs. H., an older teacher and a good teacher, was a godsend. My dubious scholastic record did not follow me, for I became her "teacher's pet." I remember walking to school one November morning and seeing the American flag at half-staff. I did not know what that meant until I got into class and Mrs. H. informed us President JFK had been assassinated. She had us watch the entire funeral. That was the gist of my remembrances of fourth grade.

Mrs. H. gave me a Valentine's card, the only one I got. She did also give one to Dick, my kindergarten tormentor, but I could live with that, even though it took off a bit of the shine.

Lorraine joyfully continued her "dumb, skinny, stupid, and ugly" mantra until it was firmly accepted into my psychic.

I moved to fifth grade. I had mastered English, spelling, reading, penmanship, Bible, geography (I love that the most), and basic arithmetic, especially successfully memorizing the Multiplication Table. I was ready to advance.

In fifth grade, we were exposed to long division. At least, most of the kids learned long division. I could not grasp the concept. My fifth-grade teacher was Miss Schlobekorn. Some of us boys named her Sarge. She was imitating a German officer, we felt. I cannot recall what she looked like, but I can recall what she did to me.

During one lesson on long division, we had examples on the board by Miss Schlobekorn, who explained it the best she could. Most of my peers got it. I did not. The carrying over to the next decimal point eluded my understanding. Little did I realize that a major hurdle in learning was that I could not actually see the blackboard well. I was nearsighted, and it wouldn't be discovered until the seventh grade. This vision deficit hadn't been a problem for me before because the preceding years I was sitting mainly in the front row. I could see the board well enough. This year, I found myself in the farthest desk away from the board, in the back of the classroom.

Miss Schlobekorn began calling students to the blackboard to show their understanding of long division. She asked for volunteers, and the smart kids like Andy, Becky, and Jeff, quickly jumped up and proved their mathematical acumen.

That was when trouble started for me. The teacher called my name. I had to walk up my row, past all the smarties, and approach the blackboard. There before me stood a long division problem not easily divisible. Larry, Mike, Dave, and Nancy were also conscripted victims. The rest of the class observed.

I stood looking at the problem and I just froze. I couldn't do it. The other kids completed their examples, leaving me up at the front alone. Eerie silence surrounded me. I felt my already protruding big ears reddening. I wanted to run away. Better yet, get swallowed up. The world was constricting on me. If I were susceptible to seizure disorder, I would have had one then and there.

Suddenly, Miss Schlobekorn was behind me, cajoling me to finish.

I couldn't. All I could do was stare at the math problem as it menacingly stared back. That's when Miss Schlobekorn slapped the back of my head and called me dumb. Actually, she may have said, "Stop being so dumb." She whacked my head again and told me to go back to my desk. A long shameful walk past all my fellow students.

I got back to my seat and seethed.

It was the first time in my life I finally became angry at such treatment toward me.

I fought back the only way I knew how. Passively. I opened my workbook and took out my No. 2 lead pencil and began blacking out the first page. Mike T., who sat to my right, witnessed my misdeed and began to do the same to his workbook. Before class was over, both of our workbooks were totally blackened out, some twenty pages, double sided.

Miss Schlobekorn caught us, and we were punished with ten after-school detentions. We had to write "I will not destroy my workbooks" one hundred times on separate pieces of lined paper every day of detention.

I did conquer long division when I was sent to summer school. But I learned that the powerful always win. It did not matter if one had a just grievance or not, because those in authority control you and will come down hard if you get out of line.

20

SAFE SPACES

I have learned two ways to tie my shoes.
One way is only good for lying down. The other way is good for walking.

Robert Heinlein, Stranger in a Strange Land

Between kindergarten and first grade, I instinctively found the secret to stave off bullying. I became a class clown, and successfully so, throughout the majority of my early school years. Being the class clown became my safe space.

I cannot articulate the process, but as a kid, somehow, someway, I learned the art of adaption to counter the bullying without becoming a bully. Laughter for me was the best antidote in warding off bullies. Through deprecating humor, I could entertain bullies by being a funny kid. I guess to them I had value in making them laugh at me or laugh with me. Bullies would turn their attention away from me to other helpless, nonadaptive creatures, such as Rosemary S., who took bullying smack in the face and paid dearly for it.

Mercifully, first grade at Christian school was a transcendent peace for me that year. I cannot recall anything remarkable happening, probably because the classroom was a safe space. Mrs. S., a kind, patient, petite woman of poster-making beauty, somehow created a safe learning environment for us overly energetic and chatty children without being forceful.

I learned to read and to develop proper penmanship. I still have in my archives some of my penmanship progress papers that she, in soft ink colors, marked my minor errors. My capital letters darted a bit too high over the lines; my smaller letters, specifically a, b, d, g, and q, seemed to wander a bit below the proper lines. All in all, good instruction without me ever feeling inadequate as a normal child in learning.

Even breaking my leg at recess that spring in 1960 did not dampen my joy of being in first grade. On that day, as during any recess during that year, I played on our school's playground, a surface of soft sand, running about, playing tag, or swinging high on the swings.

Our playground had two sets of swings, the foundations of which were made of a welded steel structure angling outward, creating strong swing sets. We kids soon learned we could swing so high that we could almost flip over the top of the swing's steel bracing (which in today's playgrounds would undoubtably be *verboden*, as would having play equipment made of steel materials). We tried to achieve this every recess, every year throughout elementary school. The girls resigned to normal swinging, not too high, but the boys, being boys with underdeveloped frontal lobes and judgments, always tried to swing to the highest height. It was terrifying and exhilarating when we reached such desired heights that we were momentarily at zero gravity, our little butts coming off the swing seat. A moment close to catastrophic demise was the goal. To add to our adolescent male idiocy, after reaching zero gravity, we slowed the swing's arc to the point we could jump out of said swing! To do it proper, we had to have a wide backswing arch propelling us into a forward thrust, launching high and out into the awaiting soft sand.

The bell rang, signaling the end of recess. I had safely ejected myself from my swing onto the soft awaiting sand when it happened. I stood up and ran back in the direction of the school entrance. A large, heavy object thudded onto me.

The thudding object was my friend Jim W., a rather stout first grader. He had jumped out of a swing, arching high, and then dropped directly on my left leg. I tried to get up. I recall Nancy B. assisting me, but as I placed pressure on my left leg, I felt as if the leg had dropped into a deep hole. I screamed in pain, pain I had never felt, even in Lorraine's beatings. I passed out, only to be awakened by adults lifting me into an ambulance. In those days, all our ambulances were funeral hearses! No EMT or fire rescue vehicles. As the professionals (actually the funeral director and employee of said funeral home) loaded me on a hearse gurney and transported me to the local Gerber Memorial Hospital, I passed out again. I awoke later in a hospital bed with a full-length white cast on my left leg.

From what I remember, all my schoolmates signed my cast upon my glorious return, and I felt special, as I had at my birthday party. I finished school and began the summer on crutches. That year, the family did not go on vacation until August.

They sent me to summer camp—"Crippled Children's Camp" at Hess Lake, Michigan. Most of the kids at the camp seemed to suffer from permanent disabilities—multiple sclerosis, spinal bifida, polio, and other physical or cognitive delays. I just had a broken leg and didn't belong at the camp because I wasn't truly "crippled." Mae was truly crippled, physically. Janet was truly crippled, mentally. She often said of herself, "I'm not off, I'm slow"—a remarkable cognition for her with an IQ of only forty-six.

I arrived at Hess Lake Camp and accepted my temporary moniker of "crippled." I liked the camp, and on its surface, it was a safe space from my family's generalized madness, a relief from living at home, and an even greater respite from Lorraine's malevolent doings. Since I was pretty much immobile, either in a wheelchair or on crutches, I was a sitting duck if Lorraine got into one of her callous dispositions. Janet, if everything remained the same, possibly took the brunt of Lorraine's moods while I was safely ensconced in camping pleasures.

Hess Lake was about a hundred-acre camp, neatly nestled along Hess Lake proper, just south of Newaygo, Michigan, and the Manistee National Forest. The camp facilities included several Adirondack cabins. There was an all-girls and an all-boys cabin with counselors sharing the sleeping quarters with us kids, a lodge, a cafeteria, craft building, an indoor roller rink, a convenience store loaded with candy and snacks, and a large water toboggan run. For normal kids, camp was a place where you could boat, tube, swim, fish, and make new friends. For us crippled kids, we could do nothing but make friends.

I met a cute girl, Suzie. She possessed a gorgeous smattering of freckles and a soft smile, and eyes which bedazzled me. She made me feel comfortable. When she smiled at me, an easy-going feeling fell upon me. I do not recall Suzie's malady, maybe a broken arm, maybe nothing noticeable at all. We enjoyed making wallets or some type of leather crafts each day. We sat together at a white pine picnic table under huge pine timber cross beams in the lodge and made beaded things, coin purses, bracelets and bejeweled whatnots each day.

She signed my cast with a heart and "Suzie" with a capital "Z" in the middle.

Every afternoon, we were allowed to go to a neighboring service station and buy candy or pop at the Hess Lake Party Store. There were no sidewalks then or now, but there was a shortcut trail from the camp to the main road. Even with crutches, I could navigate the soft trail of sand.

Camp was the only time Mom and Dad gave me any monetary allowance. I wasn't good at managing the money though, because by the third day, I had spent all the money. Suzie shared her candy. Our favorite was the Pixy Stix, a sweet-and-sour powered candy packaged in a swirly paper wrapper that resembled a drinking straw. You'd bite off the paper tip open and pour the flavored sugar powder goodness onto your tongue. I generally inhaled too soon, causing me to choke and expel the powder out in a cloud of colored sugar.

Suzie laughed. I laughed.

Every night before bed, under starry skies and stately maples and oaks, we'd sit at the campfire and consume marshmallows and roast hot dogs while camp counselors told spooky stories. Suzie sat next to me every night. We didn't hold hands but stayed close together and let each other just be comfortable.

Then camp was over. Maybe it was a week, maybe two weeks. A kid's brain doesn't comprehend time or space as adults do. But I never saw Suzie again. A sad oddity, and any chance remembrance brings back a smile or two. I wonder what life dealt her.

A few weeks later, my cast was removed, and by August, I was running and jumping and healthy again. Mom complained that we were leaving on vacation about the time her raspberries were ripening. She knew the neighbor kids were going to have free will in her berry patch. It bothered her, but it must not have bothered her that much. She wanted to see her brothers.

We went on vacation and came back home in time for me to go back to school again. I entered second grade, having more confidence in my safe space of being the class clown. The Z. boys were no longer threat, and it wouldn't be until fourth grade that I would experience peer bullying again. However, in second grade, I witnessed bullying in several different forms.

Rosemary S. was in my second-grade class. She was not pretty, and her family was not well-off. Her clothes, plain but clean, must've triggered the other affluent Christian schoolgirls to light her up, so to speak. And like a pack of juvenile jackals, the rich girls, and the girls who wanted to fit in with the rich girls, mercilessly picked on Rosemary.

I don't recall physical assaults, but that may have happened out of view from the teachers during recess. I was too busy projecting myself out of those wonderous catapulting machines called swings.

I remember sitting in class after recess, before the final bell to start class again. I saw some of the girls teasing Rosemary S., name calling and pointing out her plain clothes, simple shoes, physical appearance, or any flaws outside of Rosemary's control. They pulled on her pigtails. I thought of Mom at that point. Mom, even in youth, was not pretty or physically pleasing. Mom possessed a similar facial structure as Rosemary, a bit rounded with no distinction. Both were plain Janes, as they say. Mom herself would confess she was as "homely as a hedge fence."

I was in the same situation as Rosemary—poor and equally unattractive (Lorraine told me so). I had big ears, my left ear protruding outward more prominently than the right thanks to Lorraine using that ear as a grasp handle to hold me while she beat me. At times, girls would make fun of that anomaly, calling me Dumbo. Rosemary and I were both adopted. These similar attributes were all too obvious, and I did not want to wind up like poor Rosemary.

It was my clownish behavior that kept the tormentors at bay.

Rosemary had no such skill. School day after school day, the brow beating continued, until one day Rosemary did not come to school. Her parents took her out of Christian school and moved out of town to start again. I never saw Rosemary after that. Forty years later, I heard she had been back in our hometown to buy some shoes at a shoe store, which one of our second-grade peers now owned. It was one of his first cousins who had been one of Rosemary's belligerents. That was it, and then Rosemary was gone again.

I don't believe Rosemary had a safe space, at least not in school. Nowhere to hide.

For me, though, I had safe spaces, both physically and mentally. By the grace of God, I developed coping skills and safe spaces.

I remember Mom protecting me when I would play in the sunroom, one of my safe physical spaces in the Maple Street house. After homework was done at the kitchen table, I would play until bedtime. As a ten-year-old, I would just play and play with whatever makeshift toys I could find, like the family's Bingo game. The blue chips for the board game became the Indians and the Bingo numbered markers would be the US Cavalry. The sunroom was not heated, or only had one heat register. Winter in mid-Michigan was cold, and the single-pane windows offered little insulation. In fact, frost would condense on the inside of the panes, and I would scratch out artwork.

Lorraine, a bully and busybody, was upset that I was having fun and would always complain about me being out there during long winter nights. Mom would peek through the adjoining picture window and come to my rescue. "Oh, leave the poor kid alone. If he gets cold, he'll come out of there."

I had my sunroom and my bedroom, and Mom defended my right to those private places. When Lorraine tried to enter in or pull me out, Mom generally pushed back on Lorraine. The birthday toys incident was the only exception. Mom gave me physically safe spaces the best she could, but my safest space of all was hiding in books.

The safest place was in my own head. I imagined other places, other worlds, even traveling in my mind's eye to exotic places like Mars. Science fiction was my favorite genre, and Robert Heinlein my favorite author. I enjoyed his book *Red Planet* because I could relate to the characters, Jim and Frank. I would sit on my bed, propped up by pillows, and immerse myself. The teenage boys travel to colonized Mars, to a boarding school, where Jim's intelligent pet, Willis—a furry ball the size of a volleyball—is confiscated by Mr. Howe, the headmaster. "There are rules about pets in school," snaps Mr. Howe. Not to be deterred, Jim and Frank set out to rescue Willis from Mr. Howe's office. And the adventures began.

21

PINE REST

Once upon a time in faraway land,
a young prince lived in a shining castle . . .

Liz Braswell

I came home from school and Mom wasn't home. She wasn't in her usual spots: in the kitchen doing kitchen things or in the backyard tending to her flowers and raspberries.

"Where's Mom?"

And my sisters said, "Oh, she's visiting friends."

"Is she coming back?" I asked, receiving no real answers.

This happened regularly. She'd be gone for some time, and as a kid, like a dog waiting for its master, a moment's absence or a week's absence amounted to about the same time. Mom was gone, and then Mom was back. Mom would return and things would be unusually quiet and peaceable, but only for a time. Then bad things would percolate and reach another scorching point.

I overheard she'd visited "Pine Rest." The name held a gentleness, and who wouldn't want to frequent a "Pine Rest"? And Mom needed a rest from the rebelliousness and fussing, from the escapades of her girls staying out late or Janet running away again.

With Mom "resting," the girls were forced to cook and clean up after themselves. The cleaning fell to Janet since she was good at that, they said. Janet, wanting to please, to gain purpose or hope of recognition from her sisters, gladly obliged, cleaning the house top to bottom, washing dishes, hanging up the family's weekly laundry. The recognition never came, but the dirty laundry was constant. Wednesday was always penciled in as "laundry day." They even said it that way: Laundry Day, as if Wednesday didn't exist.

And I swear, just about every Wednesday, or laundry day, if Mom wasn't visiting Pine Rest, she would experience grand mal seizures. The incident is unforgettable, once one hears the howl of the victim: a mournful wail, long and building up quickly into a fitful screaming, writhing, and foaming at the mouth. It would occur lightly at first, usually when I was getting upstairs getting ready for school.

But I now had a purpose.

When Mom seizured, I would rush downstairs to her side as she thrashed on the floor in the kitchen or by her bedside. Between the thrashing and arm flailing, I extracted the false teeth from her mouth before they blocked her air passage. As a kid, I had quick hands and a lower center of gravity. I could get down to her side and deftly sneak my hand into her gnashing teeth without getting bitten. A bite from a person in full seizure is akin to a pit bull hanging on; there is no letting go until the seizure is complete.

At some point, after enough of these neurological oddities, Mom needed a deserved rest.

But it wasn't a "rest" as a kid knew.

Pine Rest was an inpatient treatment and dual diagnosis psychiatric center for Christians. In 1910, a group of pastors and laity decided to create an organization that treated all aspects of a person's wellbeing: emotional, mental, physical, and spiritual. Originally formed by and for the members of the Reformed Church in America and the Dutch Christian Reformed Church in America, today Pine Rest offers treatment and services to people of all cultures, religions, creeds, and ethnicities. They still reflect the faith-based heritage of the Dutch Christian Reformed traditions.

Mom would be gone for a week, maybe more. And upon her return, which I never knew when it would happen, she would reappear magically in the kitchen.

There she was again. Home. With a lethargic, unnerving mellowness, Mom turned into a Stepford spouse with that passive, agreeable look when she came back from Pine Rest. A disquieting thing, like listening to Donovan songs over and over again, sing-songing as the brain floats mindlessly, happily subdued.

But eventually, her temper came back. My friends brought her back. Her raspberries were being eaten by those damnable kids next door. The snitching of raspberries would reawaken her one passion. And by the end of the raspberry season, she went back on Pine Rest vacation.

Mom wasn't the only visitor at Pine Rest. At a Van der Weele reunion years after all the uncles and aunts had passed, I found out that a couple of Mom's brothers had vacationed at Pine Rest. And Lorraine and Janet went there too.

I never knew what happened at Pine Rest. I didn't have to. It was just that Mom or Lorraine or Janet were on vacation at Pine Rest. That was it. But what was evident was that when a member of the family disappeared, the disquieting familial environment of impending violence subsided.

The house rested. And the neighborhood relaxed.

22

COMING TO THE END OF OURSELVES

How people die remains in the
memory of those who live on.

Dame Cicely Saunders

Maple Street was closer to Henry Jr.'s grave than the old house. Maple Grove Cemetery, an exquisite plot of land situated under wide-spanning old-growth maples, had been donated to the city by the Gerber Foundation, or someone in the Gerber ancestral tree. The cemetery held magnificent mausoleums under sheltered trees and manicured lawns laid out in chronological quadrants of our small-town industrial magnates—corporate lawyers for the Gerber Corporation and one curious Italian family.

Mom purchased a raspberry-colored ceramic vase, and every spring for twenty years, she would go up twice a week with Dad, with me in conscripted tow, to attend to Henry Jr.'s grave. We rode in a '62 pickle green Ford Fairlane, me alone in the roomy back seat. I wished to be home playing with my best buddies, Gary and David, but I knew better than to talk out of turn, whine, or complain. I rode obediently, quietly watching as we entered through the black wrought iron gates and marble-sided monuments. We entered a sacred place, a place where on other days I desecrated the hallowed grounds with my friends, riding my bike, pretending to be a race car driver or a fighter pilot, laughing and shouting as kids do as we passed tombs of our Dutch first-generation ancestors and the departed Gerbers.

Mom and Dad gave me the chore of retrieving water for the flowering plants as they judiciously pulled weeds around the tombstone and added new flowers to that raspberry-colored vase. I carefully walked past impressive gravestones, flag-draped humble flat ones of veterans of foreign wars, and manicured modest ones, until I came up to the tall mausoleums of Cornelius Gerber, where I filled my gray steel water can at a spigot.

Mom and Dad waited, standing together staring at Henry Jr.'s headstone. Maybe a prayer was said. On the tombstone was inscribed a short Bible verse, "He Careth for Thee," along with a hyphen between the dates of his birth and his death at eleven years old. A short and unfulfilled life. He hadn't even had time to know God's purpose for him. His purpose for being born, then, was what? Surely, it couldn't be just to be bullied and die. But God's will be done, according to our Reformed theology; the Lord was sovereign and that was that. We will know once we reach the end of time.

Then back to the car and home again.

There were occasions when Lorraine would ride with us to the cemetery. She sat in the backseat with me. I was anywhere between seven to ten years old; Lorraine was in her late twenties or early thirties. Typically, the ride to the cemetery was peaceful, with small talk by the adults. I watched houses pass by my window, then we entered the cemetery gate, heading for Henry Jr.'s gravesite. We exited the car and made our way to the gravesite.

Lorraine did not help me get the water can filled but elected to walk around and look at other gravestones. After the usual watering and tombstone tending was complete, we'd go back to the car, Lorraine and me in the back seat.

The distance from the cemetery to our house was about one mile, or six city blocks. In that short distance, sometimes Lorraine would find something that aggravated her. And when she got aggravated, she became violent. And when restricted in the backseat with Lorraine, I would feel her wrath. As a little boy, the hellish nature of the antagonist was magnified. She regularly set upon me with great prejudice, clawing and scratching my pint-sized chest and lean arms. I still carry fingernail scars on both arms and a few on my back.

On one of these cemetery outings, on the way back, Lorraine began to argue with Mom. Dad had maneuvered the car out of the cemetery premises and up the street when I made a monumental error in judgment.

I told Lorraine to stop arguing. "Stop picking on Mom."

Lorraine turned toward me, eyes blazing fire, cursed at me, and attacked me physically. Hell is said to be like flashing fire and darkness combined, with gnashing of teeth. As the car ambled up town, back to our house, any bystander walking cheerfully on the sidewalk, enjoying a summer morning, would witness a child being beaten—punched, clawed, bitten, slapped, pinched, and kicked (whenever Lorraine had room to extend her hairy legs). My shirt suffered. She shredded it. I covered up, arms protecting my eyes and ears, Lorraine's favorite targets, if she could get at them. Turtlelike, I went into a defensive shell and bore the assaults as best as I could. This episode of violence spanned the six city blocks home, Dad blankly looking forward as the car made its way up the street, Mom weakly imploring good old Lorraine to stop beating the child. Dad pulled into the driveway, and I darted out from the back seat and ran to the neighbor's. I knew Lorraine couldn't catch me. If Dad, drunk on a fifth of whiskey with butcher knife in hand, could not catch me when I was four, then Lorraine was no match to catch me now, because I was older and faster.

I have no recollections of the aftermath. The brief peaceful interludes between these assaults seem to escape my vivid memories. I don't understand this. I would eventually go home, maybe get another round of thumping by Lorraine, maybe not, but I have no independent recollections of peaceable domicile living, just these bloody beatings. I do remember the violent interludes were part of my living in that Maple Street house. It was just an "is," a normal existence for me. That was it.

The health consequences of violence vary with the age and sex of the victim, as well as the form of violence. I had to have some sort of aftereffects, just like the passing of a hurricane leaves substantial debris and carnage in its aftermath. Back then, violence was ordinary. I learned again and again that no help would be coming. Not from the parents, not from the neighbor adults, not from the church, not from the teachers, not from anyone. No adult would come and rescue me. In time, I learned how to resist and fight back, but that was when I got older, into my teen years. And when I did fight back, the police would be called, and I would be considered the antagonist.

Life for me was bittersweet that way.

23

DINNERTIME AND NIGHT TERRORS

I have had dreams and I have had nightmares,
but I have conquered my nightmares because of my dreams.

Jonas Salk

The Chinese have a curse that says, "May you live in interesting times." It was certainly true in my home. Breakfast, lunch, dinner, supper—whatever event we gathered together to break bread, could be interesting.

Dinnertime, or suppertime as we called it, was the most interesting. At suppertime, we had the same food every night Monday through Friday for as long as I can remember, until I left home. Our menu was laid out on the stove. In a double Dutch boiler pot was boiled potatoes—just boiled, without milk or butter. Pulled from the cupboard would be canned yellow wax beans, peas, or green beans. The adults had coffee as a dinner beverage. I had nothing. For whatever reason, I was not allowed to have water, milk, Kool Aid, or any other drink. This tasteless diet continued into my teens.

Lorraine would take a giant spoonful of potatoes, chunked up and hard, and drop it on my plate (an adult portion, mind you) and then, with the same spoon, would unceremoniously drop a vegetable off to the side or smack dab on my potatoes. For gravy, they used the water from the canned vegetables. I kid you not.

In addition to the lack of culinary delights, dinnertime in my family came with an added touch of violence. On occasion, between opening prayer for the food we had and the end of dinner with a reading of Scripture, one of the aunts would make a comment, or complain, or do something that would set Mom off. Salt or pepper shakers were chucked at the unruly daughter. Mom could have been a fast pitch softball player, she was so good at flinging things from any angle. Overhead, underneath, sidearm, she did it all when she was angry, slinging any kitchen item within her reach at the perpetrator.

Once, Janet said something because she was upset. All of a sudden, a fork whizzed past my face and stuck Janet in her left arm. It hit with such force and with such accuracy that it stuck straight up and jiggled like a tuning fork. Blood oozed to the surface. Janet paused, then screamed and ran out of the kitchen, with the fork wiggle-waggling in her arm as she went out of view.

I set to finishing the yucky dinner and couldn't wait to get back outside to play with my friends. By the time I exited the house and ran down the sidewalk, I could hear Janet and Mom shouting at each other. And by the time I reached Gary's house, the event had passed over me like a summer rain, and the sun came back and the familial storm was forgotten.

Dessert was oatmeal, the consistency of drywall. The oatmeal was thick, and without anything to drink, I could not swallow it. I watched Mom put ketchup on her oatmeal, so in an attempt to try to get this nasty stuff down, I poured ketchup on my oatmeal and stirred it up, making a reddish watery mess.

The taste was horrifying. I pushed it from the table. "I cannot eat this."

But I was forced to sit until I finished. An hour elapsed. Then I had an idea. "I'm sick. I think I'm going to throw up." And I stuck my thumb in my mouth and threw up.

At that point they said, "Well, you must be sick." And they sent me to bed.

As a child, I soon learned that you can't trick adults. As I sat on my bed, famished, I learned that adults created ideocracies, fair or unfair, which we kids were conscripted to follow strictly. Protests only went so far, and rebel resistance did not end as planned.

I fell asleep with a rumble in my tummy and began to experience weird twilight hallucinations. I thought of them as night terrors, except I was wide awake in bed, trying to go to sleep. The closest diagnosis could be that I was suffering from hypnagogic hallucinations, which is the transitional state of consciousness between wakefulness and sleep. During hypnagogia, it is common to experience involuntary and imagined experiences in the form of sights, sounds, feelings of movement, or imaginary creatures.

Just before falling asleep, when the lights were turned off, I would see imaginary creatures form in the room all around me. The darkness possessed spots or dots, like twilight pixels. My eye movements would form creatures from these pixels. These creatures were mostly snake or reptilian in nature. If my eyes moved downward, they would follow, swirling in the room. And that is the moment of terror! The creatures disappeared under my blankets and crawled up my legs.

I was dead certain these creatures were real. My screams were terror-laced utterances that sent my family members rushing to my bed. It got so severe and repetitive that, out of exasperation, they allowed me to sleep with Mae. She had to lie still as I sat straight up in bed next to her and watched the reptilian creatures descend under our blankets. I would scream and kick my feet, fighting off these night creatures. Years later, Mae confessed to me that she began to believe those three-dimensional hallucinations were real because my screams were so intense.

My sisters were becoming impatient with my nightly episodes. Suggestions to spank me was their best-practice solution. If that didn't work, just shutting me up in my room and letting me deal with it was the next best offer.

Mom came to my rescue and said no to the draconian measures. "Just let the poor kid have a light on," she said.

I was permitted to leave a light on while falling asleep. That did the trick. No more reptilian monsters visiting my bed.

24

VACATION

*Vacations were the only time when
the family appeared normal, if not giddy.*

Me

Vacation meant Mom was happy one month out of the year, and early summer meant there were no raspberries yet to fret over.

We didn't vacation like most of my friends did. I never got to eat popcorn or pretzels at a major league baseball game. I never visited any national parks to eye the mighty mountain peaks in the Rockies or Cascades, or stare into the abyss of the Grand Canyon, or ride an agile pack mule down to the winding Colorado River. I never got to see an ocean or touch a hefty California sequoia or visit any coastal fishing towns. I missed out on ill-advised feeding of bears, elks, and other wild creatures, which I would only read about in my *Jr. Scholastic* magazines at school. Nor did we pile sleeping bags, lanterns, and assorted camping accessories in our Ford Fairlane and trek up north, crossing the mighty Mackinac Bridge to camp up by the rocky shores of Lake Superior in Michigan's Upper Peninsula. (Although that grand body of water was but twenty minutes from our house, I didn't see or swim in Lake Michigan until I started skipping school and partying with my buddies at Silver Lake Dunes.)

Those destinations were not on our itinerary.

Once, while in junior high, I almost visited Florida. Mae and her husband, Corwin Green, promised me a vacation with them during Christmas. Then, at the moment of embarking, with my plaid shorts and plain T-shirts all neatly packed in my little brown satchel, they reneged and left me standing crestfallen in the driveway as they drove away. And that was that, another disappointment in adults. Upon their return, they gave me a guilt offering of sorts, a stuffed alligator. Trust became a casualty in the form of a stuffed, baby alligator.

On our vacations, we visited family instead of national parks, attended colossal amusement parks, sightsaw Civil War battlefields, or walked the ramparts of Colonial and Revolutionary forts. I always wanted to stroke the glistening black sixteen-pound cannons poking over the wooden ramparts and pretend I was a Minuteman fighting the British Redcoats and green-uniformed German Hessians.

With unbridled eagerness, I packed my satchel with summer shirts and symmetrical designed shorts, a couple of Robert Heinlein books, and mismatched socks—a soldier ready for vacation. It seemed like forever before the adults were ready, but finally the time came, and all suitcases packed and secured. We piled into our greenish '57 Ford Fairlane sedan. I moved to the backseat and scooched up into the roomy back window. We were finally going.

Dad, Lorraine, and Mae would be in the front seat, Mae between them. This was in the Dark Ages of safety, without seat belts. Lorraine had to act as a pseudo seat belt for Mae. With every curve, gravity would force her to slide to the left or the right, and Lorraine would hoist Mae back into an upright position. As we set off, Mae told off-color jokes in Dutch, which made Mom smile, not demonstratively, but enough to clue us in that for the moment, sunshine and happy days were here. Here, Mom was happiest. She was going to visit her brothers.

Our vacation took us to see Mom's and Dad's families, first to Sheboygan, Wisconsin, to see Mom's brothers, and then out to the northern plains where Dad's immigration history began. Each year our itinerary changed a bit, sometimes going to Iowa first, then Wisconsin. But every summer vacation would take us to Ludington, Michigan, on the car ferry, the *SS Badger*. The *SS Badger* used to carry railroad cars, passengers, and automobiles between the two sides of Lake Michigan, linking US Highway 10 between both states. For Dad, it was an inexpensive and less hectic route, avoiding Chicago's heavy-traffic highway system. For me, it was an astounding sea adventure.

By the time I was four years old, the family vacationers dwindled to my three sisters, and occasionally a resistant brother, Gordon. Situated in the back window, I'd watch where we had been as we drove out of town, the Gerber water tower going out of view. Then, I'd slide down into the backseat, annoying the girls, and stand up by the backseat and watch Dad drive, his fedora deftly fixed on his head with a slight tilt, a cigar in his mouth, as he took us onto US 31 and beyond.

If we headed to Sheboygan first, it took an hour to get to where the *SS Badger* was docked. I got giddy when we approached Ludington; the coal-stoked smoke coming from the Badger's twin stacks could be seen as we entered the Ludington city limits. Then, and now, the *SS Badger* offers the largest across-the-lake passenger service on the Great Lakes, an authentic steamship experience. It was a cruise ship taking passengers, autos, RVs, tour buses, motorcycles, bicycles, and commercial trucks across Lake Michigan on a sixty-mile route between Ludington, Michigan, and Manitowoc, Wisconsin.

The *SS Badger* was a 410-foot-long, 590-foot-wide, 106-foot-tall ship, a behemoth for the Great Lakes. Outside it had deck areas, dining room areas, private staterooms (which we could not afford), an upper deck lounge, aft end lounge, children's playroom (not when I was a kid), gift shop, museum, quiet areas, and two free TV lounges. Back in the day, you had to put coins in to watch TV. We couldn't afford that. The capacity was 600 passengers and 180 automobiles.

Once we boarded, I was left to my own devices and wandered every nook and cranny of the ship. An adventure. I would gaze over the railings and watch the ship churn through the fresh water, dark and deep. What if I fell overboard? I was awestruck by the amount of water the ship was traveling through. What lurked beneath those waves? It was about a four-hour journey, and I spent all of my time away from the family, playing about this mighty ship.

When it arrived at Manitowoc, we waited for our car be unloaded and then we all piled back in and proceeded thirty minutes south to Sheboygan.

First stop, Mom's brothers, the Van der Weele boys.

25

THE FIVE BROTHERS

What strange creatures brothers are!

Jane Austen

As a child, I got to know these Dutchmen, visiting them almost every summer. I had a grand time with all of them—James Van der Weele, the eldest, then Johannes "Big John," Danker, Quentin, and Jan "Little John."

James Van der Weele was born July 8, 1889, as Jakobis Van der Weele, and as I recall, he was the scariest looking of the brothers. His stern Dutch look with thick eyebrows scared the daylights out of children, so said the cousins. They thought of him as mean. Maybe cold.

Cousin Ray played ball with his buddies across the street from James's house. One of his buddies would swing for the fences, the ball landing unintentionally in James's yard. Ray's buddy refused to retrieve the ball, afraid of James. Ray's buddies cajoled, "Hey, Vander Weele, go get the ball. He's your uncle."

But I enjoyed James, and maybe he had mellowed when I got to interact with him. By the time I met him, all he could do was play checkers. He had retired years before. We sat on his enclosed front porch and played for what seemed forever. James showed me tricks in checkers, like how to jump three enemy checkers in one move and win quickly. He taught me tic-tac-toe. We played tic-tac-toe endlessly, and I lost regularly. James showed me how to win in four moves, but when we played, he wouldn't let me make the first move. I gleefully took those lessons learned back to school, impressing my peers.

James was seventy-two when he died January 3, 1973. I wasn't aware of his passing until later.

Next was Johannes "Big John" Van der Weele. He was the tallest of the Van der Weele boys. I don't have many memories of him, but I heard stories about his only son, Lester, who was killed by a Japanese sniper in World War II. As the story went, Private Lester Van der Weele was on patrol in the rain forest in New Guinea. In November 1942, the Japanese were still a formidable force, and Australia thought the Japanese were going to invade their country.

General McArthur had sent the 32nd US Army

Division into a hostile jungle environment with little training. The Battle of Buna–Gona lasted from November 16, 1942, until January 22, 1943, fought by Australian and American troops. Wisconsin and Michigan Army National Guard units made up these US forces. The Allied objective was to eject the Japanese forces from positions in New Guinea and deny further use of the island as a possible jump-off point to Australia.

I often wondered what it must have been like for Lester, a young man from Sheboygan, to be thrust into such a hostile environment, all the while being shot at. It was jungle warfare. The Japanese forces were skillful, well-prepared and resolute in their defense, and had developed a strong network of well-concealed defenses. The Allied troops were severely hampered by terrain, vegetation, climate, and disease.

Lester survived the initial landings on the beachhead. One day, he was selected for a reconnaissance patrol in the dense jungle. His patrol reached a rope bridge. Several point men were halfway across the bridge when from the far side of the thick green jungle canopy, Japanese snipers began firing. Two of Lester's patrol were immediately killed. Lester returned fire, killing two snipers. But there was a third sniper. Lester died on that bridge. His remains can be found in a beautiful landscaped military cemetery in the Philippines, along with 16,558 other pearl-white crosses and Stars of David, a stunning contrast to the surrounding tropical trees and jungle shrubbery.

My uncle's only son was posthumously awarded the Silver Star. Months later, after being informed of his death, Johannes "Big John" placed a gold star in the front window of their house, signifying the ultimate sacrifice that families had paid for freedom. Lester's story was handed down, and I had often heard the tale. I later confirmed through military records the story to be true.

Several decades later, Johannes died on December 9, 1965, unceremoniously while walking along the Lake Michigan beach he had walked so often. He died of an apparent heart attack.

Danker Van der Weele (1892–1981) was Mom's favorite sibling. He was the black sheep of the family, the least conformist of Mom's siblings. Danker bought a motorcycle back in the day when good Christian Dutch folks didn't have one. He even took his future wife, Cora Gabrielse, on motorcycle rides as dates. One must understand the social culture of conservative Dutch immigrants in the early twentieth century. Having a motorcycle just wasn't a normal thing, and taking a young Dutch girl for rides, unaccompanied by a chaperone, must have been shocking. And Danker may have been a bit of a delinquent because Mom said that Danker and she once burned down trees in a fruit orchard.

My first memories of Danker were during summer vacations to Sheboygan, playing Chinese checkers with Danker at his house and Aunt Cora giving me tasty sugar donuts. Danker would be Mom's last surviving brother as I reached my late teen years. One of my final visits to Sheboygan, I sat with Danker at a dining room table.

As we sat and talked about the past, enjoying Chinese checkers and sugar donuts, he began to cry. "I'm the last of my brothers."

It was the first touch of sad emotion I had seen in any Van der Weele, including Mom. Years later, I wondered why Danker didn't acknowledge that his sister was still alive, visiting him, and had probably been sitting in earshot in the next room. Didn't she count? But as a kid, I just didn't give it much thought back then. Now, as an adult, the best I can conclude is that Mom kept a one-sided connection with her brothers.

There are photographs of one or two brothers visiting us in Michigan on occasion in the 1950s, but after that, I have no concrete remembrances of many visits by the brothers to Michigan. Only one brother attended the funeral of Mom's firstborn son, Henry Jr. Was epilepsy a factor, or perhaps her mercurial personality as she aged? She did seem to exhibit a lower intelligence along with some emotional impairment, and that may have dissuaded any reconnecting by the brothers. But every summer, we would pack up and go to Sheboygan.

Quinton Van der Weele (1894–1976) had been the first born in America. He graduated from high school in 1970 at age eighty, which made the *Sheboygan Press*. He took me swimming at the YMCA. Though he was an athletic fellow, tragically, he died of a heart attack while shoveling a late-spring snowfall.

Johannes (Jan) Pieter Van der Weele (1896–1969) was the youngest, affectionately called "Little John." Even in his late years, he sported a glorious thick head of hair, wild and free, befitting his personality. He had a mischievous side. My memories of him include watching the Billy Graham Crusade on his black-and-white TV. While the other adults were busy, he elbowed me and slipped me an open can of Old Style beer. He nudged me and gave me a wink and offered me a sip. "Shh, don't tell Aggie," he would say. We giggled and went back to watching people on TV respond to the famous Billy Graham altar call.

And those were Mom's brothers, the branches and twigs of the Johannes Van der Weele and Jennie Zweemer family tree.

Mom never had a grand mal seizure while on any vacation in the twenty years that I went with her. Her orderly brothers were good for her soul; however, they simply didn't reciprocate, rarely visiting or writing. Mom never let on about feeling slighted; she was always just happy going on vacation to see her brothers. Whether the feeling was mutual was debatable, and the brothers never let on, one way or the other.

Then westward we would go, Dad's early world next on the agenda. It would be that place, while visiting his people during those summers, that I would make a life's decision no child should have to make.

26

MINNESOTA & IOWA

Vacations are easy with "The Everything Card."

Me

Where Minnesota was the "Land of 10,000 Lakes," Iowa was the land of a million cornfields and innumerable hog farms. This vacation destination combined Dad visiting his best friend and family in Luverne, Minnesota, and visiting his sister, Pieternella Mulder, in Inwood, Iowa. The places were only an hour apart.

In 1915, Dad's best friend, Anton Vermeer, had accompanied Dad and the De Vissers from the Netherlands to America and purchased farmland in southwestern Minnesota. Anton passed away sometime in the late 1940s, but Dad remained connected with Anton's two boys, Leonard and John. Every summer we would visit them.

Leonard and John proved to be great farmers, each expanding the farmland Anton had bequeathed to them. Leonard, the eldest, amicably bought out John's portion of the inheritance, and John bought a farm only miles away from his brother. Both helped the other when needed, with haying, corn grinding, and harvesting. They remained tight-knit. Both married Dutch girls. Leonard married a gal named Dorothy, and together had a passel of kids: Eddie, Mary, Anna Mae, Jane, Marty, Burt, Beth, and Johnny. John married a pretty Dutch girl, Catherine, and sadly, they remained childless.

As we departed Sheboygan, the giant Dutch elms gave way to the western plains of short grasses and masses of cornfields. This was before expansive expressways, so we had only two-lane roads to laboriously take us to our final destination. As we left the Mississippi River basin of the Wisconsin-Minnesota state boundary line, trees disappeared, and in front of us lay only flat earth. Dad said the distance to the horizon equaled twelve miles, as we rode toward one grain elevator after another. Then another. The plains were so flat that the only object in early summer you can see of a town is the grain elevators, which every western Minnesotan and Iowan town had.

I would eagerly sit up from my backseat posture, and when seeing a grain elevator approaching on the horizon, get excited. As the silver granaries grew in size and scope before my eyes, my expectation raised my anticipation. The next town would be our stop.

"Is this Luverne? Or is this Inwood?" I would repeatedly ask.

"No. A little bit further," said Mae.

Dad just drove on, always a cigar in his mouth, his fedora pushing farther down his forehead as we followed the western sun.

In those days, it took two to three days to arrive in western Iowa and southwestern Minnesota, both a stone's throw from Sioux Falls, South Dakota. We'd pass inviting yet gaudy motels, with "vacancy" flashing in neon lights of all hues—indigo blues, midnight blue, sapphire blue, and reassuring baby blue. There were the greens—lime green, lizard green, sheen green, mint green—and poignant reds. On. Off. Then on again. Brilliant neon colors inside gas tubes in the shapes of arrows, spinning and whirling, or of reeling objects like cowboys, busting broncos, or Indians with tomahawks, all directing us off the road for a respite after a long's day's ride.

With every approaching dazzling motor lodge, I begged we stay, especially at the ones that held outdoor swimming pools and Coca-Cola vending machines. Eternity frittered inside me as the family continually passed on my expert travel advice. Finally, as the setting sun gave way to an eerie dark cast of graying clouds, we would find a motel that suited the adults, cheap and with no outdoor pool. Their tastes for lodging differed greatly from my own. A motel with a pool and a dancing cowgirl in a provocative skirt would have been nice, but too expensive, Mom muttered. Lorraine thought the sign was risqué and awfully sinful.

One summer, we did stop at my motel choices. It was when Mae's husband, Corwin, drove us to Iowa. Dad was getting up in years, and Corwin took over the driving. Corwin had purchased a new beige 1966 Chrysler Fury III station wagon, roomy enough that I had the entire back portion of the car to myself.

I could watch the semi-trucks and give them the signal to honk, a fun pastime for a kid. The truckers would honk at me when I gave them a train conductor's arm motion. Another game I played was to call out all the Ford Edsels, with their distinctive front grills, that I spied. I devised these simple pleasures when I discovered I couldn't read while riding in a car. The first time I tried, I got car sick and Dad had to immediately pull off to the side of the road. Of course, his incessant smoking of cigar stogies didn't help my tummy.

Corwin bragged about a cashless society and proudly exhibited a wallet full of credit cards: Chevron, Texaco, Sinclair (the one with a green dinosaur logo), a Goodyear (for tires), a Sears card, and one card he announced as the "Everything Card." With this array of cards, we traveled in class. Corwin made driving interesting with his certain gas station credit cards. Back in the 1960s, gas stations were not as plentiful as they are today. As we drove through these remote, two-lane roads, most gas stations were positioned in the sparse towns and villages. Corwin would always be close to running out of gas because he would only stop at the service stations whose credit cards he held in that burgeoning wallet.

He enlisted me to spot upcoming Chevron, Sinclair, and Texaco stations, and if there were no locations in one city, he would drive on gas fumes to the next village. He was good at calculating the odds of not running out of fuel because just when I thought we would be stranded, the gas gauge on "E" for seemingly miles, he would find the right station. In my mind, it was a wonderment. We never ran out of gas, but I swear we ran on empty for a portion of our drive through Iowa.

One vacation, Corwin got to use his "Everything Card."

I recall packing my suitcase and proudly carrying it to the Fury III, setting it at curbside along with all the other family gear and travel cases. Lorraine and Corwin loaded the luggage into the vehicle, Lorraine hoisting up the luggage to Corwin, who secured it on top of the Fury's luggage rack. Once the luggage was loaded, we set off for Iowa. I could almost spurt burst with intense expectancy—another adventure out west with the Vermeers.

When Corwin drove, we no longer went to Wisconsin first, but through Iowa to visit Dad's sister, Pieternella. The adults stayed with her, and I was dropped off at John and Catherine's farm. We arrived at the first stop in eastern Iowa, a quaint motel, and one with an outdoor pool. We unpacked the luggage. I waited impatiently for mine.

It was gone. With the other luggage present, there seemed no way mine could have blown off.

Corwin said, "I packed all the luggage good."

I was crestfallen. As with the way all my birthday toys from my only birthday party had disappeared, now my favorite summer clothes, my only belongings, had mysteriously disappeared. Corwin reassured me not to fret as he took me into town and bought me all new clothes with his "Everything Card." He and he alone accompanied me to the local Sears store and bought all the summer shorts and cool button-down shirts I picked out, with that magical plastic card.

Mom frowned and Lorraine grumped, but Corwin declared it was no big deal. "The kid needs clothes, for gawd sakes," he affirmed.

It became my favorite vacation travel-wise, and it solidified my endearment toward Corwin to the day of his death. In addition, he brought order into the family, and Lorraine became less violent toward me.

Corwin racked up the entire vacation on credit cards. And unbeknownst to me until years later, he never paid them off!

Every journey through Iowa was tedious for a young kid. It was flat and sparse of anything exciting. But generally, in two days we reached Iowa's northwest corner, Rock Valley, Lester, and finally Inwood. My understanding of maps and geography was limited, and with every approaching city, village, or town, I thought it was our final destination, a distant grain elevator suckering me in, again. The error usually occurred in the middle of Iowa, when we still had three hundred miles to go. Sooner or later, we would reach our western destination. Finally, on one of my umpteenth utterances, "Is that Luverne or Inwood?" I would receive the hoped-for reply.

"Yes," Mae said with a grateful sigh.

My wiggle became full-bodied as I stood up in the backseat and stared out the front windshield between the shoulders of the adults up front.

Almost there.

And "there" meant a world beyond all worlds. White farmhouses with large porches; great red barns surrounded with sheds that neatly stored farm equipment—corn grinders, cultivators, manure spreaders, hay wagons, discs, plows, seed planters; and the adjacent pens that housed pigs, cows, chickens. An orderly world. If we arrived to Inwood, Iowa, first, then Dad was visiting his sister, Nellie, now a widow. If Luverne, only thirty or so miles from the Iowa state line, then to visit Dad's best friend, Anton Vermeer, and his kith and kin.

Anton passed away before I was born. Like many retired farmers, after years of hard days of farm chores, Anton died shoveling snow, having succumbed to one massive heart attack.

As a child, I had several of my classmates lose their farming dads in a similar fashion, resting in a chair or going to bed and never waking up. My dad went the same way years later. Farming was a dangerous occupation. Many a farmer met their end through horrific farming accidents—like catching a sleeve in a hay baler and being pulled into a grisly death, or having a farm tractor tip over and crush them, leaving them to die alone. Dad, Anton Vermeer, and his two Vermeer boys, also farmers, all died either in their sleep or shoveling snow. A gentle ending to a redeeming occupation.

When we arrived at the Vermeer's farms, I couldn't wait to hop out of the car and be allowed to have a farm or two to explore. As a child, I didn't yet know how Mom and Dad visualized the farm. Farming had been a way of life; then, through calamities not of their making, they suffered intensely bad experiences.

Mom's and Dad's intent was different for me.

I believed we were on exploratory vacations, joyous escapes from city life to a world of creatures I only read about in books. Of splendid steers, bulls with hefty horns, giant pigs (650 pounders!) and endearing piglets squealing, free-ranging chickens, ducks, and geese. A rooster actually crowing in the morning dawn. The smells of farm invading the hosts' homesteads. The homes had the scent of fresh, warm milk and animal feed. A delight to me.

Visiting friends and family was my parents' secondary purpose, and I was unaware of their primary objective, which would not manifest itself until way into my adult years.

27

THE VERMEERS

Farming looks mighty easy when your plow is a pencil
and you're a thousand miles from the corn field.

Dwight D. Eisenhower

My recollection of Dad's best friend, Anton, was his strong, redden face, granite-like cheekbones, and guttural broken English. Anna, his wife, spoke more Dutch than English and possessed a tough exterior, which curtailed my excitable behavior when in her immediate presence. Anton and Anna moved into town upon retiring to a nice house in Luverne by the water tower. Anton died shoveling snow on a February day. He was only seventy.

They had two boys: Leonard and John Vermeer. Leonard had a large family of seven children by the time

I made my appearance. Several of the children—Marty, Barbara, Burt, and Johnny—were near my age. I had heaps of fun with Leonard's kids, and I would see them annually up through my teen years. I felt they were the cousins I never had. We had so much fun playing in the yard, exploring the farm, fishing a nearby stream, and riding bikes on the dirt roads past massive fields of corn, wheat, alfalfa, and soybeans.

Leonard's and John's farms sat on the former grasslands of the Northern Prairie. Now, cornfields pushed out the grasses that had held back droughts for eons. We kids didn't know that, we just enjoyed being kids, riding bikes under a big sky, the horizon sprawling and alluring. I wondered where it would lead. I breathed in deeply the smells and sounds of prairie farm living with the Vermeers. I relished those summers.

Leonard's family was like *The Walton's* TV series. Suppertime we gathered at a great table that sat in the middle of the kitchen, loaded with bowls of mashed potatoes and green beans fresh from the garden. Fresh milk in glass pitchers adorned both ends of the table, and heaps of fresh sweet corn, a large bowl of mashed potatoes, fresh tomatoes, and chicken filled up the supper table. Leonard's and our family all at the table included sixteen hungry souls.

Laughter and lighthearted kidding covered the conversations, so unlike dinnertimes at home. It was great fun listening to the adults joke and carry on, spoofing one another. Eddie gently teased Lorraine, and Lorraine laughed, loving the attention.

I enjoyed Leonard. He was John's alter ego. He swore as much as my mom, whereas John only said "shucks." Leonard may have drunk more than coffee, but John didn't drink at all until Catherine died suddenly from an aneurysm in 1980. Only then did I find hard liquor in his house, which was a shock to me.

On one of those weekends, sometime when I was still a preadolescent, I found myself going to church with Leonard's family. I recall the sermon was about swearing. The preacher had four sermon points on swearing. (All Dutch preachers were taught at either Calvin College Seminary School or Hope College, both in Michigan. Every sermon needed sermon points. The template evolved into four sermon points, with the sermons lasting excruciatingly forever in a child's mind.) He somehow made a distinction between blaspheming, cursing, cussing, swearing, profaning, and taking the Lord's name in vain.

I was moved by the sermon, and all throughout this spiritual discourse, I gazed at Leonard, knowing full well he had successfully accomplished in expert skill all the categories of bad language that this preacher expounded upon. I knew Leonard even took the Lord's name in vain when an inanimate farm implement gave him grief. Maybe the preacher had been at Leonard's farm on a Christian charity call.

The preacher reached Leonard. His spirit must've been convicted because I noticed a somberness about him. I couldn't wait until service was over to get Leonard's take on this most piercing homily. As we gathered outside after church services concluded, I walked beside Leonard and bluntly asked what he thought of the sermon.

He looked down at me. "Yopi, don't buy into everything a preacher says."

And that was that. No remorse, no spiritual conviction. Leonard was not only unmoved by the four detailed sermon points, he had a defense.

I took Leonard's outlook to heart and began to have what I thought to be a healthy distrust of clergy, or at least of homilies and sermons. And after that, my opinion toward Mom's utterances changed. I looked upon cussing, cursing, and swearing as no more than a different language, a kind of guttural cleansing of the soul. I began to loosen up my language.

From my fractured childhood recollections, my family turned me over to Leonard's younger brother, John, and then at some point, my family headed back home, leaving me with John and Catherine for the remainder of the summer. John was a handsome, robust, red-cheeked Dutchman. A second-generation farmer, he adopted the same lifestyle of prairie farming as his father, Anton. Both boys were fantastic farmers. Leonard, making a good living off the land, was able to send his daughters to college. Anna Mae became city clerk for Luverne, Minnesota, and Mary became warden in an Arizona state prison.

John married a nice-looking Dutch girl, Catherine, but soon discovered they could not produce children. So, Providence apparently provided me for John and Catherine, at least as far as all the adults were concerned.

Every summer from age three to fifteen, I found myself spending a good portion of my summers at John's and Catherine's large farm. I played on that farm, pretending to be a cowboy fighting bandits or Plains Indians. I helped with chores. Up at the crack of dawn, dressed in farm overalls, I would rush into the kitchen, push up to a silvery aluminum-sided Formica kitchen table, and have a large farmer's breakfast of fluffy, buttered pancakes, fresh bacon, and warm cow's milk, directly from the barn.

John would listen to the commodities report on the radio. He had already milked cows by the time I was being blessed with protein-filled breakfasts, the likes of which I never experienced back home.

John softly laughed as I gulped the warm milk, frothy cream covering my upper lip. "Now you have a mustache," he kidded.

I laughed.

After breakfast it was out of the house with John to gather eggs and feed and water the chickens.

Catherine was a stern young woman, rarely smiling.

The only time in my decades of knowing her that I recall one smile, and a quick one at that, was when she presented me with a watch for my thirteenth birthday. We were driving in their car, me alone in the backseat, when Catherine handed me a present. I unwrapped it and shouted with glee at seeing my first wristwatch. My excitement and honest joy must have stirred her too. When I looked up, Catherine was still peering at me from the front seat, and a soft smile came across her face. I never remembered her smiling like that again.

Aside from the wristwatch-giving episode, I never felt comfortable around Catherine. She wasn't mean or abusive, just disciplined and stern, her humor a side note only when in the company of adults. It was as if she thought that if she let her guard down in front of children, it would break the needed veil of authority between adult and child. If that veil were torn a bit, then the order of familial things would break down. Stern dispositions by adults unnerved me. But a silver lining— she didn't beat me or stuff me into tight, dark places.

Yet I needed smiles. Warm smiles.

I learned to do chores, watering and feeding chickens, gathering eggs, and filling water troughs for the hogs, cattle, chickens, ducks, and geese. Gathering eggs was a daunting task for me as a little kid. I had to gather eggs from chickens that were nesting in two-tiered nesting boxes. Feisty hens did not respect the little hands of a child when egg gathering. John gave me a red wire basket and modeled how to reach in under a nesting hen and push her back to reach under and grab the eggs. I did as instructed, reaching underneath the hens and fetching warm eggs.

Most of the hens were compliant, squawking a bit in useless declarations as we stole from them, but there were a few nasty hens that showed no respect The joy of successfully retrieving those fragile oval treasures changed quickly. Seeing my hand reach up toward them, their heads raised up in a posture of potential aggression and they clucked loudly, warning me to back off.

"Show them who's boss," John said in a chuckle. "Like this," he said, reaching his big farmer's hands under the irritated pronouncements of the most annoyed hens. He easily pushed up a hen's underbelly, taking out several eggs. He made it look easy.

Yet my tentative behavior didn't fool those hens. I was not boss.

The surliest of hens, a fat white Rock Island hen, nested in the top nesting box, and I had to reach up and under her. This didn't bode well. She knew the difference between John's hands and mine, and she pecked me. I tried again. Again, she rose up, bad-tempered, and pecked me. Every morning that same bad-tempered hen pecked my hand. Luckily for me, these laying hens had their top beaks (the pointy, sharp part) snipped, so the pecking never drew blood, just startled me. In time, I knew the good (compliant) hens from the bossy hens.

I carefully placed these warm eggs in my red wire basket and brought them to Catherine. She took them to the basement, washed them, and placed them in a cooler. Unlike store-bought eggs, some of these eggs were brown, with an occasional light blue.

All of farm life was a wonderment to me. Farm chores gave me order, which I hadn't experienced in my familial environment and which paid dividends in my adult life. It also gave me some semblance of self-esteem. When I got back to school, I could hold my own with the farm kids, talking about the finery of farming out west.

I would feed and fill the hog water trough. I hopped on the wooden fence which penned in the hogs.

"Don't fall in. They'll eat you, skin to bones," said John. He told of a relative who had been feeding hogs and fell into the hog pen and was eaten then and there. If the intent was to frighten me to be careful, it only gathered my courage to climb higher and peer over and watch these domestic monsters. Other times, I would bend down and stick my hand between the fence rails and attempt to scratch a pig behind the ears, maybe scratch its back. It was amazing to feel such coarse hide.

"Don't get your hand near the snouts," John warned. "They bite. Look—" and with that, John would grab the nearest squealing pig and lift its upper lip, exposing large front and lower tusks, three to four inches in length. "Razor sharp too. Take a child's juicy finger clean off."

There were times John had to take grain to sell at the Sioux Falls stockyard across the state line. That was intensely exciting for me. Thousands of steers and hogs were penned, awaiting slaughter at the Morrell Meat Packing Company. It should have been more of a sensitive thing for me, all these animals going to market to be made into nicely packaged bacon, steaks, pork chops, and roasts, but in my mind's eye, this was just another "is" I was born into. The slaughtering of these animals was disturbing, but it was a reality beyond my control and a necessity in the grand scheme of living. I had helped Dad slaughter a hog before, so a dulling at seeing this had already begun.

John took me on one occasion to tour the packing plant. The poor beasts were garnered into pens just across the street from the packing house, then crudely shepherded through a tunnel underneath the street into the slaughter rooms on the other side of the street. It was best described as a massive assembly room.

Visitors were not permitted during the actual slaughtering phase. We entered an area above the slaughter floor, where the animals now hung on hooks, upside down, blood already drained. The carcasses passed us on the conveyor belt. It was a reverse disassembly system, on a mass production scale. The evisceration continued as the carcasses were sent down the line to employees dressed in bleach-white overcoats, white hairnets, and masks and ready to perform their specific duties:

dismantling the creatures until there was nothing left but the empty slaughter hooks. The now empty hooks disappeared behind a plastic curtain on the conveyor system to pick up more slaughtered domestics. The tour guide boastfully stated, "We waste only the squeal." A chuckle followed, and the visitors followed suit.

The final part of the tour took us to the actual packaging of all the animal products and by-products, ending next to a massive steel machine called the "Weenie Genie." The nonpremium beef and pork parts entered one end of the Weenie Genie and out the other end came hotdogs. Visitors were invited to take a hot dog and partake. Most passed on that, but I didn't. A free hotdog was not to be passed up. I grabbed a hotdog, which less than an hour or so ago had been an air-breathing creature. Somehow, I compartmentalized this act and had no moral compunction as I gulped it down.

Should the scenes inside that packing plant have played more in my head? I can't say. Now that I'm an adult, I have an honest attitude toward the eating of meat, but not in the same manner of vegan zealots. I say a prayer of blessing for the animals that had to be made into meats for us. When I pass a cattle or hog truck taking the animals to market, I say a prayer for them, asking the Lord not to forget these creatures but to bless them into the New Heaven and New Earth I believe to come. It may seem silly, but the Lord knows my prayers are deep felt and offered up.

The stockyards were less disturbing, but once when John took me to the Sioux Falls stockyard, I was chased by a large angry steer. We were walking between pens as permitted, me a few steps behind John, when a gate was opened and steers were released. They bordered down the chutes to another pen, and we had to leap to safety by climbing cat-quick up a side corral fence.

John laughed a belly laugh and complimented me on my agility.

He made me feel good.

28

I'M A BIG FARMER

*Agriculture is the most healthful, most useful,
and most noble employment of man.*

George Washington

John had all green John Deere tractors and one gray metal utility Ford tractor, which had a front-end bucket. He would allow me in the bucket and sharply raise it up and down, herky jerky—a kind of roller-coaster feel to it. I laughed and jiggled, and below me I saw a wry smile come about him. We had fun.

John had lots of tractors and cool farm implements. He had an A and G and MT and a 50 John Deere series tractor, the ones with small tires in the front, similar to a tricycle. He also had a Series B in the grove, which he used to grind corn, a loud process that I helped with. I should be deaf, as the corn was so loud when it went into the PTO-driven corn grinder. We didn't have earplugs back then. I could have been killed too. One slip, one moment of not paying attention when shoveling the corn into the grinder, and you would slide to a grizzly end. It happened to experienced farmers, farming being one of the most, if not the most, dangerous occupations in the world. But there I was as a twelve-year-old, shoveling corn with a real farmer on a real farm, living dangerously and deliciously. I breathed it all in totally.

John trusted me to drive a tractor. He had me sit up on his lap behind the wheel of a G series John Deere and showed me how to operate the levers and pedals. He drove the tractor as it *putt-putted* through the barn yard, past the pasture of his contented cows grazing beyond the barn next to an expansive cornfield. We arrived at a corn cultivator setting at the edge of the field, where he demonstrated how to hook up the tractor to the cultivator, how to raise and lower the cylinder discs, and how to maneuver the machine between the rows.

"Be careful when reaching the end of a row," he said softly. "Turn wide after clearing the row; first left turn it, then sweep right and the tractor will bring you back to the next rows without smashing any corn stalks." He demonstrated as I remained on his lap. His big arms enveloped me as he took the steering wheel and spun the tractor out of one row and into another row. "That's all there is to it, Yopi."

He and Leonard had always called me "Yopi," and to this day, I do not know the meaning of that name. I do know it was an affectionate nickname and I came to love its sound. *Yopi.*

John hopped off the tractor, waved to me, and walked back to the farm, leaving me alone on top of this great, shiny green farm tractor with an equally impressive farm implement connected to it. The tractor idled, waiting for its next instructions.

With adrenaline flowing, I put the John Deere G into gear and pushed the accelerator lever a tad. The tractor responded, now *putt-putting* faster. John Deeres, in those days, all had exhaust pipes sticking straight up from the engine mount, and for reasons not known to me, had a steel cap affixed to the top of the exhaust pipe. When the tractors engaged out of neutral and accelerated, the steel cap would bounce up as the exhaust was expelled. The faster the tractor went, the more the steel cap would remain erect.

I loved watching the diesel smoke pour out of the exhaust pipe and *poppity-pop* that cap. I guess it is a boy thing, because when I later had a son, he saw a large diesel dump truck go by us as we were walking down the road and blurted out, "I love the smell of diesel, Dad." My daughter and granddaughter never liked that smell. Now, my grandson gets the shakes of excitement when Grandpa starts up his Yanmar 324 utility tractor.

I tentatively let up on the clutch, looking back for John. He was almost up to the barn, his back toward me. I was on my own. A preteen city kid on a farm tractor, alone out in the great prairie land, cultivating sixty acres of cornfield! The cultivating took all day, but I got it done, with John's approving gestures. At the end of the day, we finished the daily chores together, had supper with Catherine, then sat in the living room to watch the nightly news and future weather reports. I felt good accomplishing something, and having an adult, especially an adult male, tell me "job well done" was invaluable. I believe at that moment, I became less like a lost kid and more like a valued young man.

John became the closest thing to a positive role model for the rest of my life. The remainder of my years, no other adult male affected me in such a positive manner. And if I had thought deeply about our relationship, I would have thought of him as my dad. I could have made farming my occupation, upon introspection. But things turned out differently. There were some unsettling moments that may have changed my mind as I got older. It was the life-and-death struggles of farm animals. I experienced firsthand one disquieting attribute about chickens while staying with John and Catherine.

As I was feeding the chickens, I witnessed a sick hen out in the pen. Her feathers were unhealthy looking and molting. The other chickens were periodically attacking her. If she came near the chicken feed or water trough, the other hens that were already there would peck at her head, even trying to get her eyes. I told John.

He said, "Oh, she is sick and will probably die."

"Are we going to help her?" I asked, feeling emotionally disjointed.

"Nothing to do but let it go. It's just the way it is. Chickens sort things out," he said.

The next day or so, when feeding the chickens, I noticed the sick chicken was dead. In the middle of the pen, some loose feathers lay strewn about. I grieved. I couldn't do anything, could I? Why didn't John rescue her? He had enough space he could have given her a safe space, sequestered her so she could get better . . . or at least try . . . but he didn't. John didn't even consider that. I would have rescued her, but I was only a little kid, not even in the second grade. Emotionally unflustered, John didn't help that chicken. In my mind, he at least could have secluded her from the other hens, couldn't he? Then she would not be tormented to death.

I determined that I would help those sick chickens or other helpless creatures when I could. I took that to heart. And to this day, I am empathic to anything or anyone weak, helpless, or sick. I have befriended vulnerable creatures to the best of my ability and limited means; I have broken up dangerous fights between men, to my own possible peril, and I have protected abused women in several violent situations, even to the point of endangering my own life.

We live in a fractured world, a broken and I daresay depraved world. Although God knows our thoughts and actions, and even though He desires for us to choose wisely and to seek direction from Him, the natural order according to our circumstances plays out. God watches but doesn't intervene. I am reminded of Henry Jr. and that sick chicken. Just like the other chickens henpecked the sick chicken, did the other kids know that Henry Jr. was internally ill, aware in a sick chicken kind of way? Did Henry's peers bully him, did they push him down that flight of stairs? God allowed it, but I know in my heart that God disapproved mightily of their actions.

I now adhere to an internal precept that God expects His children to defend those in a state of weakness. He expects his children to defend them when confronted with scenarios such as what happened to Henry Jr. Where were the children of God when Henry Jr. was bullied? Why did they not stand up and stop it? Maybe they were the bullies.

An uneasy and disquieting spiritual struggle ensued in me after seeing that poor sick hen. I wasn't judging God. I was judging us. I was also judging me! I could not take back what I saw or heard as that little boy.

I learned to handle death on the farm. Aunt Catherine, as I began to call her, had me help butcher chickens, and I became somewhat morbid in that process. She had me catch them, which was fun for a kid, chasing around an enclosed chick coop, where the unfortunate chickens could only circle about as I cornered them. I don't recall any emotion, as I knew their fate. I'd catch them and hand the squawking bundles of feathers to Catherine, whereupon she would dispatch them quickly by laying them on a stump and chopping off their pecky little heads. She would release the now headless chickens, and I would watch in awe as they ran around, blood spurting straight upward, sometimes crashing into another headless chicken if Catherine was fast enough in the dispatching of more than one chicken at a time. They'd eventually come to rest. Maybe that was the comeuppance the healthy hens had coming for being mean to sick chickens.

On occasion, John and Catherine would let me spend a couple of weekends with Leonard's family. I had a grand time with Leonard's kids, especially Burt, Johnny, Marty, and Barb. The fraternal twins, Marty and Barb, were my age. We played on the farm, pretending to be cowboys and Indians or sheriffs and bad guys, or wrestling in the front yard. Burt, being the oldest, always won. But he was gentle when pinning me in a headlock, and he'd quickly let me go.

We'd find ourselves at the back of the house in

a large, untended raspberry patch. It was a wild and leafy entanglement with raspberries hidden deep in the bushes. We'd push the branches apart to uncover the big, delicious berries. I was about to clutch some of those hidden berries when I saw movement near my hand. I had almost grabbed onto a large fruit spider! It was the largest spider I had ever seen. I backed off in horror. Michigan didn't have such a creature. It was as big as my two hands together. I'd swear his eyes, all eight of them, locked onto me. It was a raspberry spider, a large, black arachnid with giant red eyes on the abdomen, and something as big as the size of spiders I read about in *The Hobbit*, as Bilbo entered the bleak forest of Mirkwood. I jumped out of that berry patch and never returned.

John had fun with me. He was a kidder and enjoyed playing pranks. Once, when we went to the Sioux Falls Stockyards in his big red grain truck, I noticed the GMC logo on its front grill.

"What does GMC stand for?" I asked.

"Great Mountain Climber," he said, straight faced.

I took this as gospel. When I returned to school that fall, I bragged to my buddies about riding in a Great Mountain Climber. They hooted and belly laughed and, recovering from their collective guffaw, enlightened me. GMC stood for General Motor Company. What a funny guy, that John.

On another occasion, John and I were out in the

pasture feeding the steers. I had to pee. Farm boys peed where they stood. "See if you can hit the top wire on the fence," John said.

I aimed and delightfully arched the stream onto the top wire, the one connected to electric insulators. Immediately I felt a shock as if I'd been bit by a stinging insect. I was thrown back and gave an accompanying yelp. I had hit the electrified portion of the fencing.

John laughed. "Don't believe everything someone says," he said, "not even friends and family."

29

BETRAYAL

Trusting you again gave me more pain.

Garima Soni

As a kid, I enjoyed those carefree family summer vacations when we visited the Vermeers. I was in my fifties when I was informed of my family's true motives for those summer vacations. According to Mae, the spokesperson of the family who recounted the story to fill in the gaps, I was set in front of John and Catherine and my family when I was four or five and asked to choose between the two families.

When I heard this, I was shocked. I do not recall at any time having to choose a family, pick a destiny. I couldn't believe my family wanted to jettison me. I was the best thing for them, I thought. I grew up and took care of many of them in one way or another. I had their collective backs. I chose Mom and Dad and all the failings accompanying that family. I elected for a known commodity of chaos and abuse rather than a seemingly idyllic farm life with loving adults.

There in the middle of the Vermeer kitchen, two sets of families positioned me. I do not recall how the exchange actually went, but it could have been:

"John and Catherine want to adopt you. They want to be your new mommy and daddy," Mae might say. "Wouldn't you want to live with them?"

"All the time?" I might have said.

"Yes. Wouldn't that be fun? Living on this farm?" Mae said.

"No!"

"No?" family members chimed in.

"No! I want to live with you and with Mommy and Daddy."

John and Catherine may have employed some coaxing, but maybe not. They may have stood around the kitchen table stoically watching the drama play out, or maybe sat at the Formica table with red and silver trim, dessert and coffee on the table as Mae coaxed the issue.

"No!" Stress probably entered my voice. Maybe I cried and tried to climb up on Mae's wheelchair. Maybe I hugged the side of her chair, the cold steel side with the March of Dimes sticker stuck on it.

That scene in Catherine's and John's kitchen never reached my impressionable threshold. Luckily, as a child I remembered only enjoying the vacations, and not the sordid details. I thought everyone was enjoying the same world as I saw it. Thinking now of the time Mom and Dad took me back home with them, I realize it must have been a disappointment. They must've meant well . . . for me and for them.

Yet the not knowing what really transpired in those summer vacations now grips me with sadness. I was wanted but unwanted. I chose to live with people who possibly didn't want me.

After I rejected the Vermeers, they eventually withdrew from me. The vacations out to Minnesota became more erratic, sometimes only lasting for a week, no longer a whole summer. Upon introspection with adult eyes, I realized I had hurt them and it had become difficult for them to see me as when I was a child. When John and Catherine passed away, I was not written into their will. I was not informed of their deaths until sometime after they were buried. There were no photos of me with them in those golden days; only one photo was sent to me ten years later, and upon request. It was a grade-school picture of me that Mom had sent to them, and it sat by a clock in their living room. No photos, I was told, of me with them. No photos of me playing on the farm. No photos of feeding chickens, cows, or pigs. No photos at all.

What did I do to estrange myself from the Vermeers? I was a good boy. Maybe a bit excitable, as one great-aunt described me, but isn't every child excitable? If not, then maybe that child has issues. What were my issues that warranted being socially jettisoned by John and Catherine? Did they harbor lasting resentment for when I chose my known family over them? Did they really expect a child that young to make such an earth-shaking decision? What might my life have been like had I chosen to live with John and Catherine?

I continued to visit both Vermeer families every summer for fifteen more years. I hold joyous memories of those summers, of farm chores, of haying, of learning to use a farm tractor, of learning everything about farm life, and yet, unknowingly, I had probably caused an emotional schism with every adult and created enmity with the only people I had ever loved and bonded with.

Maybe that was best—not knowing—because, as an excitable boy, I thoroughly embraced those summers with great zest.

Yet later, the knowing gave me great pain.

30

NORMA

I stopped outside a church house
where the citizens like to sit.
They say they want the Kingdom
but they don't want God in it.

Adam Clayton

My family lived a mile away from the church. On Saturday night, the bell would ring a couple of *bongs*. Did the church bell annoy close neighbors?

Norma lived a block from our big Dutch church, and every Sunday at 9:00 a.m., 9:25 a.m., 7:00 p.m., and 7:25 p.m., she heard the church bell clanging. No other church bell in Fremont matched its sound quality. When it rang, it didn't chime like the tintinnabulation of wind chimes or a collection of smaller bells—it burst into a rich baritone *bong! bong! bong!* that could be heard miles out of town, a clarion call to worship. It was a magnificent church bell, as church bells go, weighing over four hundred pounds and made of cast bronze. The rope connecting to the church bell was tightly woven rope, thick as a Dutch farmer's hand. As kids, it took two hands to firmly grasp the rope and two of us kids to tug at it. We couldn't make the clapper touch the side of the bell.

Despite Norma living close to our church congregants, we were cultures apart from Norma and Alex, her husband. Unlike us, Norma was not a churchgoer, was not Dutch, and was not a Gerber. She was, whether by design or happenstance, a social outlier. Both she and Alex were poor, bedraggled, and grimy in appearance, even when they were clean.

Norma and Alex lived in a gaudy two-story faded-purple house with wood siding that stood at the corner of Dayton and Steward Street. It was the town's eyesore. I always thought of it as a witch's house since it resembled a haunted house. Best way to describe the porch was as standing on chicken legs. It needed massive repair as the enclosed porch was at an odd tilt. As I walked to school or to church, I imagined Norma as a witch flying out of the purple monstrosity of a house, grabbing me with long witchy fingers, and swooping us back into the house before neighbors would be the wiser. The kitchen had to be dank and smelly, children's bones piled in the corner, I thought.

Yet I was mesmerized by her scary appearance and erratic behavior. With a child's curiosity, I would find myself edging up to Norma's house and listening to their domestic quarreling. I could be caught, and that added to my contradictory eagerness. If caught, would Norma beat the crap outta me? Maybe grab me, drag me inside, and throw me into a preheated oven and cook me alive? Was she just waiting for curious little boys like me to come so she could have a tender child roast? Those were my wild thoughts.

I heard Norma yelling at Alex from inside, the crashing of dishes or kitchen implements accompanied by a symphony of expletives and guttural cussing at Alex. The caterwauling sounded like my world. In that moment, as Alex was receiving familial justice, I felt relieved.

Ours was not the only crazy house in town. Maybe we were a bit odd, but not as much as I perceived.

I saw Norma beat Alex, then he stumbled out of the house onto the tilting porch and quite marvelously navigated down the street, out of the range of the flying pots and pans. Norma continued her verbal assaults from the front porch. Alex mumbled and wibble-wagged his way around the corner, heading uptown and out of harm's way. I took off as soon as Norma came onto the porch. Couldn't get caught and be eaten.

It was behaviors like that which tagged Norma as crazy and, everyone presumed, certifiably drunk nuts. And, adding to that moniker, Norma was scary looking. I thought she was a witch for she looked like a witch, having no fine facial features, unlike the sexy witch, Elizabeth Montgomery, of *Bewitched*, Mom's favorite TV show. Norma was more akin to Baba Yaga, the Slavic witch in Russian folklore, a supernatural being who appears as a deformed woman who steals, cooks, and eats her victims, usually children. Norma had the girth and gait of a Bulgarian weight-lifter, with arms to match. She moved quickly, almost supernaturally, in that bent frame of a body. She was a ferocious-looking woman even when cleaned up.

Townsfolk were disinclined to associate with Norma, even for a friendly hello. When she came uptown, folks subtly grabbed their children and slid to the opposite side of the street, fearing she might engage in conversation. Norma had the north side of Main Street all to herself. People who talk loudly to themselves while meandering city streets tend to dissuade folks within the range of normal to cozy up and say hello. And Norma certainly talked to herself as she walked to the IGA grocery store daily. People surmised she was schizophrenic. Norma would only buy a small amount of packaged food at IGA, then disappear back toward the purple house, or be seen on the road east of town.

I asked Mom about Norma. Mom said, "You be nice to her. She has her own troubles." And that was all Mom ever said of Norma, even if I persisted in the inquiry. It was as if they were kindred souls on the road of suffering, both on the way to the eventual end of themselves. Norma apparently wasn't a witch, I could safely assume after my brief dialogue with Mom. I left it at that—be nice to Norma, which led me to want to get close to Norma.

And one day I had the opportunity. I witnessed Norma going into the IGA store. I crossed the street and heard her muttering softly. "Hi, Norma," I bravely said.

Her muttering stopped. She looked around until she saw me standing by her side, smiling. I hoped she didn't see the shock and fear of being that up close to her, for it was still a fright for me. "Hi," I said again.

She peered down at me, not saying a word.

I thought of running away, screaming bloody murder. Mom would not have approved of that.

Norma just stared at me. I smiled and repeated my overture: "Hi." I threw in a trump card, hoping that would protect me now that I was in grasp of her scary claws. "My mom, Agnes, says hi too."

Then it happened. Norma smiled back. It was as if the greeting had reset her humanity and but for a moment taken her out of her tormented mutterings.

I noticed she had soft eyes. Eyes like my mom's, just as sad if one looked closer.

A hello back, then she went into the IGA store. She didn't even try to eat me.

All my friends thought I was quite courageous for coming within an arm's length of Norma. But I found Norma fascinating. She must have had a story to tell, but I was too young to know that then.

Our church had missionaries in Nigeria, Sri Lanka, South Pacific Islands, and Brazil, yet God did not call a single elder or deacon or pastor to mosey over one block and reach out to Norma and Alex. Weren't they a mission field too? In that purple house lived two hurting souls. Were they not children of God, as well as those in distant lands? Why did my church and other churches in town ignore these two people?

When addressing this epiphany of Christian oversight with Mom, all she said was, "A wonderment, isn't it?"

On occasion, I witnessed Mom and Norma together downtown, talking, but that was the extent of our physical contact with them. Mom later told me Norma's history. She explained Norma's raging at Alex wasn't without just cause. "He drinks away his paycheck the minute he gets it." That left Norma to live on her meager Social Security check. "She has to take care of her father, too," Mom said.

Norma's father, Russell Giles, depended on Norma for things. Her dad was blind. He had been blinded while serving our country overseas in World War I. Russell had been a member of the Michigan regiment. "He is an honest-to-goodness WWI veteran," Mom explained. He had been in the same American Expedition Force as Dan Gerber. Both had served along with the French in the Argonne Forest. Russell had been wounded, possibly by shrapnel, leaving him permanently blinded.

During the 1917 campaign, Dan Gerber had been a scout for the army. His missions were to cross over enemy lines and capture German soldiers. These captured soldiers would be a wealth of information about enemy battalion strength, any signs of morale breakdown, or weakness in the enemy's lines. On one such mission, Dan crawled up to the German lines and somehow captured two German infantry men and one officer! Imagine capturing hostile soldiers then forcing them to crawl back with him through no man's land, all without them signaling for help from fellow German soldiers. He brought the prisoners back without incident, a remarkable feat!

After the war, Russell and Dan returned home with no fanfare, Russell now a wounded and blind veteran.

Dan Gerber's dad, Cornelius, was a successful industrialist in our town, a self-made man, building up a successful tannery and then a booming canning company. Due to his heroics, Dan Gerber was well received after the war. The city leaders set up a homecoming celebration for Dan. A podium was set up in the middle of town under the new clock overlooking the new bank.

On Main Street, the podium sat with red, white, and blue ribbons and decorations adorning the corner. A "Welcome Back, Dan" sign hung between two buildings on the corner of Main and Division.

The townsfolk waited for Dan to give a rousing speech. Dan Gerber ascended the podium and gave his speech, descended the podium, and walked home. Years later, his son, Dan Gerber Jr., asked his father, "Do you remember the speech?"

"Yes. Word for word."

"What was it?"

Dan Sr. said, "I'm hungry and I'm going home."

Mom claimed Russell was a war hero too. He had fought bravely during several battles and was blinded during one of those battles. The exact details were never known, and Russell remained in a VA hospital in Grand Rapids, Michigan.

Norma would visit her dad every week, bringing him special treats or food from that IGA store. Rain or shine, snow or sleet, Norma hitchhiked some fifty miles one way to Grand Rapids several times a week to visit her dad, until he passed away October 18, 1978.

When I got a car, I would trek to Grand Rapids and look for Norma. But by the late 1970s, I never saw Norma hitchhiking. I didn't see her downtown anymore either. I did not know what had become of her. I wonder if any church folks driving along those Michigan highways had picked her up. I'm hoping so.

Town gossip had it that Norma had killed her husband, Alex, with an axe. Dan Gerber, Jr. professed that is what he had heard.

She didn't. Norma passed away before Alex. I found their gravestones. Norma's grave lay next to her husband, Alex Jules. Her father, Russell Giles, rested on her right, Alex on her left, both marked with American flags denoting military veteran. Alex had been a WWII veteran, with an honorable discharge. I hadn't known that until I recently found their graves. He died October 27, 1980, a year after Norma.

Norma's gravestone simply read: NORMA DAUGHTER 1921–1979. How strange for that poor gal. Even in death she was neglected, with no last name. Turns out Alex and Norma were never married. Why didn't the funeral home give Norma a last name? Why not Giles, as it was her dad's surname? Who was her mother?

Upon her death, the church, or a wealthy congregant, bought her house at a nominal fee, demolished it, and built a fine single-family ranch, making a tidy profit. To the delight of many, the neighborhood now looked presentable.

31

RASPBERRY WARS

The raspberries...have always been here (for the whole eleven years I have owned but have not owned this house), yet I have never tasted them before.

Erica Jong, "Raspberries in My Driveway"
from Becoming Light: Poems New and Selected

Unlike her brother Danker's raspberry patch, an expansive two hundred linear feet, Mom's raspberry patch, which butted up to the neighbor's side of the garage, was a smidgen smaller at twenty linear feet.

Danker's wife, Cora, was concerned that the raspberries shouldn't go to waste. So, she divvied out the raspberries to the needy and to the local restaurants as her cash crop. I believe she used some of that money to help pay for her youngest son, Ray, to go to Calvin College.

Mom's vision for her patch was a "don't touch" approach. Her smaller raspberry patch yearly produced an appealing bumper crop of deep red and black fruity delights. The patch was thick; its flowers blossomed in the spring and offered themselves up to the bees, and by summer, the raspberry bushes produced brilliant black and red raspberries, hairless and delicious, begging to be taken and delightfully eaten. Mom refused to pick the fruit and forbade all of us to pick the raspberries, as if the patch were the holy of holies. And it wasn't for the birds because she wasn't that bird friendly. She just did not want the raspberries picked! We never had raspberry jam or jelly or raspberry pie or any dessert connected with raspberries. We had enough raspberries, I believe, even with the twenty linear feet patch. But I cannot recall one quart picked.

In a messy sort of way, she was like her brother, Danker. He recorded his quarts of raspberries picked, but he had no idea the purpose of the record keeping. He just wanted to have some kind of record. For Mom, there was seemingly no purpose to her vigilance. She just didn't want anybody to pick those raspberries. "Neighbor kids are always picking my damn raspberries." That was her lament.

Fresh fruit was scarce within the confines of city living. Back then, most moms canned fruit bought at the local family grocery store. No one else had vegetable or fruit gardens, only lush, manicured lawns that we kids found great delight in rolling and tumbling in. The neighborhood parents seemingly didn't mind the host of twittering children running unrestrained throughout the neighborhood. The exception was our yard. None of my friends were allowed onto our grasses. If I wanted to play with my friends, I had to go to their houses, play in their yards.

And definitely no kids were allowed to partake of Mom's raspberries. Mom's prohibition only enticed my friends to violate her ordinances. Her angst happened when she witnessed any kid on her property, especially in the backyard. It became a daring do, an inviting taboo for my neighborhood friends. The temptation was too great. My friends raided the patch early and often.

From our back porch, as a child, I watched the neighbor kids sneak behind the garage and pick Mom's raspberries. Mom witnessed the thievery, and every summer while we lived on Maple Street, began her raspberry war. To set the stage, the belligerents were my friends: Gary and his brother, Greg; neighbors Paulie, George, Dave, Guy, and his sisters, Renee, Tammy, and Jackie; and Jane and her brother, Steve.

Mom set against the neighborhood children, and the moment the first raspberries ripened, Mom willfully ensconced herself in front of her kitchen window and surveyed her small raspberry patch. From early morning with her first cup of coffee, she looked out the kitchen window, surveying her backyard. If all was copacetic, she'd sit down and enjoy a cup of coffee. She would wash dishes, clean the kitchen, and make lunch, always with an eye toward the raspberry patch. When Mom witnessed my friends sneaking into the backyard, she would storm out onto the back porch and give them a "what for." She cussed and shook her fist toward the patch, shouting and threatening the little buggers, and the kids scattered. It was akin to chasing crows out of the orchards.

Luckily, she didn't know how to utilize a shotgun, for she'd probably have no moral compunction about discharging the weapon in the air over their heads. But we didn't own firearms, so she stuck to launching livid invectives at my friends in both English and a vanishing Dutch dialect, which came out in a guttural sound. That did the trick. The kids scattered to the four winds, but, like crows in the fields, they would come back and the scenario would repeat.

Summer on Maple Street then was rarely peaceful. From the very first ripe raspberry to the end of the raspberry season, Mom fought the neighbor kids, herself, and sometimes me. I'm not even sure she knew that I was stealing the raspberries too. The neighbor kids were all my friends, and I was caught in the middle of this localized community conflict. My alliance shifted between my marauding friends and Mom, depending on the circumstances. If I was in the house doing homework or doing other chores, I would passively align myself with Mom. During her tirades on the porch, I remained inside, conveniently quiet.

But there were many occasions where I would join in with my friends. When we got bored of doing other things in the late summer, somebody would say, "Hey, quick, let's go get the raspberries." I could have said, "No, that upsets my mom." But I didn't. There I was, an accomplice. There I was, mute. I was a follower and marched right behind them, going up the back way of the Mendham's house in their backyard and behind the garage.

We ten-year-olds were pliant and flexible and able to soldier-crawl up to the raspberry patch, grab the low-hanging fruit, and scurry back to safety. It was the raspberries that were further up the plants that we couldn't resist; those berries exposed to the sun grew plumper and tasted juicier.

Gary, the next oldest after me, became the main belligerent. He'd entice us to follow him around the garage and go directly in front of the berry patch to stand and pick. Gary seemed to have an internal clock and knew when to pick and when to slide back to the side of the garage unobserved. He was like the bad kid in school who knew just how to sass a teacher and when to stop, just before the teacher would lower the boom. I often marveled at his impeccable timing. He was rarely caught.

But, by the time the second or third courageous kid tried it, Mom spied them and came out of the house, screaming and swearing at them. Often, the kids would scurry away in fright. However, on some occasions, they would scamper back to the safety of the Mendham's property and laugh at my mom.

I didn't laugh, but I didn't support her either. I regret that to this day. There on the back porch stood Mom, alone in her fight to protect the one and only possession she could control, and I just watched my friends mock her and treat her as less than she deserved. I was the oldest of us neighbor kids, yet I did not act like I was the oldest. I let Gary lead. I was a follower. I easily could have admonished my pals, yet I allowed them to taunt Mom—a haunting inside me to this day. They mocked her and I did nothing. What was wrong with me? I live with that regret. Even now, when I think of those times, I feel sad. I didn't have Mom's back.

Maybe that's the lesson I learned. Maybe that is what I needed to learn to become a better person—to act and stand up for others even if you don't understand their ways. I would like to believe that Christ helped me see this, or at least He has given me the sensitivity and courage to stand up and be counted.

32

THE CANDY CLOWN INCIDENT

The Big Noise from Scottville.

Scottville Clown Band

Mom was generally disinterested in social events and would only be seen outside tending her garden or driving with Dad to the cemetery to water flowers at Henry Jr.'s grave.

On occasion, when we other family members would upset her, she would head out the front door in a huff and storm-march uptown, muttering all the way until she reached the Caruso Malt Shop. There, she would order a strawberry sundae and sit alone in a high-back booth, sheltered away from everyone. A moment of turbulent loneliness.

Her daughters never pursued her. They let her go.

I was in my early teens when I witnessed her storming out of the house. I was too young to have any effect on bringing her back or accompanying her, in case the worst would happen—a seizure. Looking back, I feel saddened because I did not place myself in her shoes. What was she feeling in those isolated moments? Aside from a possible grand mal seizure, Mom could incur an insulin reaction from ingesting a strawberry sundae, due to her diabetic condition.

She avoided social gatherings with the exception of attending church services. But she made an exception for one particular event—the local parade. And I was ecstatic because the Scottville Clown Band would be in the parade.

The Scottville Clown Band's roots date back to 1903 when the Scottville merchants decided their boring free-trade business world needed a bit of spicing up. Originally, these merchants began to dress as hillbillies, eventually evolving—or devolving—into fashionable, more risqué costumes. They entertained the local carnivals. Then World War II happened. The colorful merchants put aside their bawdy self-fashioned costumes and brass-sounding instruments and went off to war to defend the world against evil empire-building dictators.

In 1947, Scottville merchant Ray Schulte reformed the group and recreated what is, to this day, the Scottville Clown Band. He would say, "It's one of the highlights of my life." He would become the godfather of the band. Most people do not know that the band is also a nonprofit, granting thousands of dollars in scholarships for education in music and performing arts through the Raymond J. Schulte Music Scholarship Fund.

To date, they still tour festivals in Michigan, such as the Lilac Festival on Mackinac Island, National Trout Festival, Cedar Polka Festival, Irons RV Park Show, Manistee Beach Show, Troutarama Concert, the USCG Festival Parade, and the not-so-famous Mackinac Island Dog & Pony Parade. And when I was young, the Scottville Clowns visited our town annually for the Fremont Old Fashioned Day Parade, which was held the third weekend in July. Fremont began having an annual celebration in the 1950s as Fremont Old Fashioned Days, but in 1991, the festival changed its name to National Baby Food Festival, to honor Dan Gerber, a leader in the baby food industry.

The biggest day of the festival was Saturday, highlighted by the Gerber Products Company Grand Parade and an ensuing firefighter's water battle. The firefighter's water battle would take place at 2:30 p.m. on Main Street, a grand spectacle in its own right. The parade generally began 10:30 a.m., featuring almost one hundred entries, including the newly crowned National Baby Food Festival Queen and her court, an array of floats, marching bands, color guards, entertainers, and clowns with the Scottville Clown Band.

The sporadic arrival of the amusement rides at the beginning of the week—and the arrival of the AJ Carl Show—would jinn up my excitement. I rode my bicycle to the city outskirts to see the staging area at the county fairgrounds, a scouting mission of sorts, taking a gander at the carnival trucks to see what new rides were coming to town. On Wednesday, the carnival trucks moved into town in wildly colored semi-trucks sporting clown faces, bawdy logos, and risqué sketches of unrefined women. The trucks offloaded on the city park grasses, disgorging rides like the Scrambler, Loop O' Plane, Ferris Wheel, Tilt-A-Whirl, and my favorite, The Paratrooper.

Along with the amusement rides came the additional money makers—concession stands advertising every sort of french-fried and deep-fried edibles known to man, and dubious carnival games set up on the side streets, ready to vacuum coinage and dollars out of every young man who would take a date to the festival. You could spend a week's wages on a $2 stuffed animal, which a lucky date could parade the remaining evening. Thursday night, the rides would open with discounted tickets.

Friday and Saturday mornings, Main Street merchants emptied their stockpile of products—clothing, shoes, and garden tools that hadn't sold—and held sidewalk sales. Tables sagged under mish-mashed clothing piled in unruly mounds with yellow sale signs as jazz tunes blared from speakers above rooftops. The store fronts presented shoppers with a kaleidoscope of homespun capitalism. Folks came out thick as a locust cloud to gather sidewalk-sales goodies, the very things they turned away from 363 days a year.

After the event, all of the unsold items were shoved back into the stores, giving way to the heralded Old Fashioned Days parade, as if the parade was the Lord's Supper of capitalism. Townsfolk would be blessed in the partaking of parade watching, reverencing the good old days. Anything from the 1920s and Depression Era was revered and found worthy.

Mom rarely attended sidewalk days or anything related to our town's festivals. Maybe her epilepsy scared her away from crowds. The commotion of so many folks milling about downtown stores might stimulate a convulsion.

During Old Fashioned Days in 1961, Mae met and married the operator of The Paratrooper, and therein would begin a whole new chapter in my life as I entered my teen years. His name was Corwin Green, and he would knock our familial world off its already wobbly axis. Corwin would be the bringer of newfound freedoms, and for me, outlandish escapades. His insertion into my world would make a perfect storm, fraught with danger, but also a bastion of new experiences. He would, by proxy, teach me the nuances of the world, a world apart from responsible people's standard of uprightness.

Friday through Saturday evening, AJ Carl amusement rides growled, swirled, dipped, and rumbled beneath the maple trees in the city park. Giant generators resounded, sparking life into these adrenaline-encouraging machines. It was electrifying, and the noise and lights enveloped me, a welcome break from violence and family traumas. Lorraine claimed the music was "devil's music," the lyrics blasting tunes with implied sexual seduction. But I saw it differently. I fell in love with the rhythmic guitar licks of Credence Clearwater Revival, John Fogarty's bayou-growling voice piercing my soul with music so different from the pious and cheerless Psalms of our church's Psalter hymnal.

I was losing my religion, and, in its stead, picking up another.

We held a great parade, with old-fashioned farm tractors, a 1908 steam-powered combine, vintage cars, floats, marching bands, miniature ponies with monkey jockeys, and our fine fire department. An occasional clown melted with the crowd, throwing candy and making animal figures with colored balloons. And of course, there was the Clown Band. Onlookers bemused at these clowns' hairy arms in summer sleeveless dresses and other bawdy, clownish clothing. Patrons claimed they came to see the clowns for their musical acumen. We kids came to see their antics and their racy gyration in choreographed splendor—twirling and blasting their trumpets, attired in flowing feminine garments of every hue.

Mom and I were sitting curbside in front of the De Kuyper-Visscher Men's Clothing Store. We had front row seats. The newly erected analog clock donated by the Gerbers and prominently hung at the corner of Division and Main Street, above the Old State Bank (Dan Gerber Sr. held his corporate and philanthropic meetings in the upstairs room of the bank), said it was 98 degrees. On that hot, mid-July Saturday, we watched the floats, the vintage cars, the fire trucks, the marching bands, and the floats.

Then came the Scottville Clowns. I heard them from blocks away. My neck stretched as I looked back down the parade route. Then I saw them, in marching band formation, attired in uncoordinated colors—a bright canopy of happy lime greens, sunshiny yellows, flamingo pinks, and assorted polka dots. Leading the Clown Band was George Wilson, the band major, carrying a toilet plunger colored like a barber's pole as a makeshift baton, with an extended handle for dramatic effect. George exhibited in orange-and-yellow-checked bib overalls and matching top hat, leading the clowns in tight military formation. The band, dressed in full regalia of spicy outfits and form-fitting sundresses on masculine physiques, played horns, trumpets, tubas, piccolos, and flutes, marching proudly and resplendently while blasting tunes from bygone years—jazz, boogie-woogie, and big-band stuff.

George twirled his toilet plunger with the artistry of a drum major, chest forward, high-stepping past us.

He was quirkily majestic. His smiling, happy clown face greeted us. Cheers went up. A miniature train with linked cars wiggle-waggled in front of George and his clown troupe. Robert J. Schulte was the train driver, dressed in matching checkered orange-and-yellow suit coat and slacks. He snaked the train through the street. A clown flotilla on minibikes circled the band in figure-eights.

Then came the Candy Clown.

Candy Clown moved back and forth, covering each side of the street. He carried oodles of taffy candy in oversized front pockets, and with his white-gloved hands reached in, grabbing handfuls and whimsically tossing hard candies willy-nilly toward the curb, toward us kids. Kids scrambled into the streets, grabbing the candy as if they were pieces of gold. Had the clown tossed dimes and quarters, I'm certain the adults would have mimicked the kids.

The Candy Clown approached us. I was ready to catch some candy when it happened.

A hardened taffy in a purple wrapper tied at both ends flew, at what I presume was the speed of light, and hit Mom squarely on the forehead, just above her wired-rimmed prescription glasses. In slow motion helplessness, I watched it hit Mom in the face. Mom charged Candy Clown, blaspheming—and not just in English. Expletives flew in Zeeuws, a fluent obsceni-ty-laden display, as Mom moved in on the clown. Mom picked up the offending purple projectile, and any candy not yet touched by kid hands, and sidearmed the candy back at the happy Candy Clown.

The Candy Clown saw a purple wrapped taffy soar past his face. Then a few more candies hit him. He turned and faced this fluffy old woman in a flowered dress barreling at him and mouthing f-bombs. Surprise turned to wonderment at the illogical scene.

An old lady was attacking him.

Then, as with an F5 tornado coming in massively and quickly ascending back into the clouds, Mom tired and stopped. Her internal organs, racked by years of unregulated diabetes, limited her energy. But that didn't subside her bilingual obscenities. She pushed through the crowd, her flurrying arm gestures signaling her fury the astonished crowd, who gave way, allowing her wide berth, knowing she was still in dangerous mode. Not caring what spectacle she had created, she stamped home.

Mom never went to a parade again.

The parade was on a Saturday. Mom went to church on Sunday, forever hopeful that the Lord would eventually lift His hand and give her relief. Was relief too much to ask? Peace might have been out of the question.

Nine years later, she found peace. I was there to witness that day.

33

TAKE IT AS IT COMES

Everyone who wants to do good to the human race
always ends in universal bullying.

Aldous Huxley

During my teen years, new variables burgeoned. Mae married and moved away, and from an influx of testosterone and Lorraine's continued malevolent presence, I lost joy. I began to allow my circumstances to determine my level of being.

As I entered junior high, my state of being became a state of unhappiness, which led to frustrations, which led to anger, jealousy, and the worst state of being— entitlement. By the time I reached high school, the physical manifestations became alcohol abuse and violence.

When I entered high school, the bullying had changed. The bullies' circuit now centered on boys who came from broken homes. The perpetrators were usually four-lettering athletes trying to impress the cheerleaders. Thankfully, public school teachers were restricted from whopping upon us unregulated and squirming boys. But I had to adapt. I had to figure out the best practice to avoid getting the crap kicked out of me between classes or in gym class, because I felt naked, vulnerable, and afraid.

It would be a fight between two bullies that unknowingly helped me.

On a sunlit autumn day, Danny T. beat the bejeezus out of Terry Q. There at the corner of Main and Division, in front of the steps of Griechen's Women's Wear store, Danny and Terry faced off. These were the two toughest kids in school, aside from Kenny B., who terrified me. I had front row seats to this event. This was an equal fight, and my first experience watching a real fistfight. My previous experiences centered on me fighting Tommy K. in Junior High, with Tommy and me wrestling and harmlessly punching with winter mittens on in the middle of the teachers' parking lot after school hours. No one was really hurt, and afterward, Tommy became a longtime friend. In time, we held Bible studies together as young adults during the hippy Jesus Movement, and even started a non-denominational church with real hippies who came in our town.

The other event close to a fight was in sixth grade with a peer, Clyde B. Somehow, I had irked Clyde, and he squared off with me. He challenged me to a fight. Now Corwin, an avid wrestling fan, had taught me how to defend myself a la big-time wrestling style, running and jumping at the opponent like the famous Flying Fred Curry. I knew that would not bode well. I visualized flying through the air, legs out in front, Clyde dodging off to one side and me falling on the ground helpless, where Clyde would pounce on me and whop on me until, mercifully, an attentive teacher would break up the beating. The specter of Mom retelling Henry Jr.'s death due to being bullied rested on my shoulders as Clyde and I faced off. I was now past the age of eleven, the age when Henry Jr. died, so I felt secure that this moment of facing a bully would not end in my death.

Clyde raised his arms, fists clenched in standard boxing stance, and continued to challenge and berate my lack of courage. I stood there in complete contemplation. At school, I never slugged anyone. At home, I had allowed Lorraine to pummel me as I gained acumen in protecting my head and vital parts until the beatings subsided. This was different. Clyde wasn't family, and I was not going to be beat up by this kid. I was not going to be bullied.

Clyde dropped his elbows, exposing his face. I took a swing and punched Clyde square in his nose.

A right-handed, straight-arm extension with a closed, bare-knuckled fist square into his nose.

Clyde buckled as his nose began to bleed. "Why did you do that?"

"You said let's fight," I said. "So I did."

Clyde ran off to get a teacher while I stood perplexed. And that was the end of things.

Now, here on Main Street, real fisticuffs were brewing. There were no adults to stop it. A learning experience presented itself.

Danny was lanky, and Terry solid as oak. Neither had fought each other, saving their pugilisms for the less fortunate school victims who pissed them off. These were alpha predators. Even the jocks wouldn't fight these guys. Each of these boys seemingly had their own turf. It was unwritten but we kids all knew the boundaries. Terry generally hung around the arcade hall down by Fremont Lake, and Danny held the downtown arcade and pool room, named the Purple Haze. Somehow, Terry had ventured, foolishly so, into Danny's marked territory.

Planned, ordained, or by happenstance, the two squared off, and we knew these two weren't backing down. Had we been betting kids (being a Calvinist, betting was forbidden), we might have laid bets. I would have bet the money from my paper route with 2:1 odds it would be a tossup.

What wasn't expected was Danny beating the bejeezus out of Terry. And in less than a minute. Terry struck first, leaning in with a right punch. Spider quick, Danny arched his back as Terry's fist connected with clean village air. Danny counterattacked, throwing a left then a right, connecting with Terry's left cheekbone, then the right side of his head.

Terry's head moved backward as his crumpled one knee slid off the curb. As Terry tried to recover, Danny was on him, throwing punches as Terry helplessly took blows to his head. Terry collapsed, slipping off the curb and partly under a Ford Galaxy 500, four-door sedan. Danny bent down and lowered several more blows then backed off, waiting for Terry to be dumb enough to ask for more.

Terry didn't. He looked up. He held up his left hand in surrender fashion as Danny stood over him. As soon as it started, it was over. And, as Terry picked himself off the street and sheepishly went out of view, I learned the finer points of protecting myself. The fisticuffs between Terry and Danny taught me that I didn't have to take a beating anymore. I could fight back and give a beating.

I began to practice the art of boxing. I bought boxing gloves from Frank's Sporting Goods and petitioned my buddies, Dave and Gary, to be my sparring partners. They declined. So, I turned to real fighters. One was a Christian-school friend, Kelvin D. He was a tough kid, but he and his bigger brother, Barry, always treated me kindly. The brothers thought me an entertaining class clown, and Kelvin and I found ourselves in many an impish school escapade. I asked Kelvin to box. He eagerly accepted.

We faced off with my new boxing gloves in the front yard of another buddy's house. In attendance were Guy R., Gary, and Dave. It was to be a fun practice engagement. I started it off, slow-punching at Kelvin's gloves, which blocked his face. A feeling out of sorts. The punches then began in earnest, solid movements with power transferring through the torso and legs, pivoting to gain full-force impact. Kelvin blocked every punch. Then everything went black. The next memory I have is of Kelvin standing over me and asking if I was okay. He had knocked me out. A weird experience. I never saw his right hand come full force into my jaw.

Undeterred, I continued boxing and fighting lessons from an even more formidable foe, my teacher and neighbor, Steve L. Rumors claimed Steve was a Golden Gloves boxer. Steve was short, stout fellow. He was twenty-one years old and known as the coolest of the cool guys in our town. He drove a deep blue Malibu muscle car. High school girls were always riding in the front passenger seat as he cruised town. The backend of the Malibu was jacked up and had a racing carburetor, which growled coming up to street intersections.

When I lobbied Steve to teach me effective boxing techniques, he readily agreed. He suggested his parents' living room when his parents were not home. It was agreed. Gary and Dave volunteered as referees, or sadistic onlookers. Dave and Gary moved the furniture around, creating a pseudo boxing ring. A living room couch protected the picture window. When all was squared up, Steve and I faced off.

I was petrified but equally excited to enter into this experience. I was learning how to protect myself beyond hiding behind my comedic class-clown persona. Being funny, even with self-deprecating humor, had lost its effectiveness in avoiding the bullies' beatings. My humor wasn't helping in the high school environ. Bullies just wanted to fight and prey upon susceptible schoolmates. My humor only led to more fights, or potential fights, which up to the point when I faced off with Steve, I was ill prepared to win.

Steve started off the lesson with a punch to my stomach, a soft punch with an accompanying laugh. "Elbows up," he said, "but bend your waist to stop body blows."

The lesson went well, with soft punches and instructions on counterpunching.

Dave and Gary sat waiting for a good lesson.

Finally, Steve said, "Okay, let's go!"

Micro lessons complete, I now had to see what I learned. We moved off makeshift corners, and Dave gave the signal for a real boxing match. Exhilaration beyond description flowed though me. I was boxing a Gold Gloves fighter. We moved toward each other, boxing gloves raised, fighter stance ready. Steve allowed me to introduce my first learned left-right punch. Elbows up.

Steve responded with agile counterpunches, lightly initially, but with a bit more energy than earlier. I bounced and ducked and pivoted and felt confident, punching Steve, going for the face. He blocked every attack, but I blocked his counterattacks.

Then, somehow, I connected with his face in a right-handed punch, hitting him slightly off the jaw.

His eyes grew angry. "Counterpunch!" He gave me a flurry of attacks, which sent me on my heels.

I could only block his blows. I swung wildly, forgetting my lesson, and dropped my elbows. Steve threw one punch, and I found myself flying backward, hitting the wall that divided the living room from the kitchen. He hit me again. My torso broke through the drywall. I sat stunned. The kitchen lay open in full view. I don't recall Steve's reaction, but Dave, Gary, and I boot-scurried out of the house.

Steve never mentioned the incident, except to critique me a bit. "You kept your elbows up, but you have to stand and counterpunch. If you keep eyes on the fists not the face or eyes, then the counterpunches will work."

With that, I felt proud. Bullies didn't seem as terrifying any longer. Destiny was no longer in others' hands. I controlled my life from then on.

Admittedly, I entered tenth grade with a chip on my shoulder. I remembered the stories of Henry Jr. being pushed down a flight of stairs and Mom claiming that is what killed him—suffering kidney damage from the fall. Nobody was going to push me down any stairs, let alone bully me. Physical confrontations generally occurred or were incubated between classes. The hallway crowded with students rushing from lockers to the next class, and the jocks and cool kids felt this was a grand time to exert their status in the pubescent pecking order. It might start with a bump, a push, or a look. Maybe nothing initially, but the incubation period was set.

At least for me, I responded first with a steely maligned squint, locking eyes with the perpetrator as we passed through the crowed hallway. Nothing would happen at that moment, and I would go to class, find my seat, tuck my books under the seat, and allow the bump to simmer in my brain. By the end of class, I had a fomenting gripe toward said student, and if that student came close to me again—and of course, he would since we had to pass through the hallway seven times in a school day—I would teach him a lesson.

I fought with the cool kids, the jocks, and the rich kids. I was in the group labeled "hoods," which stigmatized me as being poor or a user of drugs, or both. I got into many fistfights, and most of them ended in my losing since I was of much smaller stature. Some kids called me "mad dog." I was fine with that moniker. A tough reputation can lead to a more peaceful existence.

By the end of tenth grade, I had been in enough scuffles to earn suspensions, which led to my resistance to educational institutional authority. I came late for first hour, or didn't go to school at all, electing to pass school hours at Purple Haze. The Purple Haze was downtown, a block or so from the high school. It was owned or operated by an elderly man we called Pops. The instant you entered the Purple Haze, you would be labeled a "hood," forever affixed to that lower-tier clique. Good kids didn't venture in.

To my knowledge, not one of my Christian-school friends ever entered that facility. The place was dimly lit with psychedelic lights. Cigarette smoke darkened the room. Pool tables, pinball machines, and ratty chairs made up the decor. There was a stage toward the back door area, where local rock-and-roll bands played Friday and Saturday evenings. A staircase just inside the front door led up to a small balcony area, where the only light was a small second-floor window on the street side. Only the real "hoods" went up there.

I eventually did and found it to be a convenient place to buy pills and drugs. In the late 1960s and early 1970s, the high school cliques were primarily made up of seven types: Preppies (rich or privileged kids), Jocks (athletes), Stoners (a.k.a. Hoods), Nerds, Muscle Car Guys, and Partiers. I attest the microcosm of my small town pushed me into the Stoners (Hoods) group.

The fights diminished by the time I reached my senior year. During high school, and for the majority of my life, faith in the Lord took a backseat as I absorbed unexpected bad things like a duck waddling through a stormy day, shaking off the water, to go about its business of survival. I no longer saw life as rainbows and skittles but more as thorny wild raspberry vines, minus the raspberries. Mom had taught me to look at life expecting the bad things that would be coming. A joyless outlook, but one in preparation for future surprises.

It's a funny thing what our eyes see and how we allow bad things to get in the way of joy. Now, I see there were many blessings and many fortunate outcomes, even during what I thought were bad downturns in my life.

34

THE FUNERAL

Now everything mattered so much,
the here you can return to, the now you never can.

Dan Gerber from A Voice from the River

It had been five years since I graduated from high school when Mom's biological kids decided Mom needed to be placed in a nursing home. I was still living with Mom and Dad, feeding them, giving them their medications and insulin injections daily. I would go to work, and on noon breaks, come home and ensure they had lunch. Arriving home one lunch hour, I found Mom lying unconscious under the bathroom sink.

I knelt and attempted to awaken her. No response. She was comatose. I knew she was in a diabetic coma. If she didn't receive medical attention soon, she would die.

Dad sat unmoved in his favorite chair, staring off into space, showing no emotion.

I called for an ambulance.

The ambulance transported her to the Gerber Memorial Hospital, where she remained in a coma for a day or two. The prognosis was not good. Her treating physician stated that once a person went into a diabetic coma, it was difficult to recover. But on day three, she responded, recovered, and was out of danger.

While she recovered in the hospital, the family, aside from Dad and me, decided Mom needed more care and needed to go into a nursing home once she was released from the hospital. I was not consulted, even though I was now an adult and her primary caregiver. It didn't feel right to see Mom in the nursing home, but Dad's inaction when she slipped into a coma was troubling. I asked Dad, "Did you see her fall?"

He didn't remember.

"Why didn't you call an ambulance?"

He said he didn't know how to use the wall phone.

"Why didn't you go to the neighbor's?"

No response.

So, Mom was placed in Newaygo County Medical Facility for the aged. It didn't feel right, but with few options, I was resigned to see Mom leave her home, never to return. The other family members were resistant to helping, claiming to be busy with their lives.

Mom hadn't been institutionalized for long when I was informed by family members that the police had taken her away to the state hospital in Traverse City, Michigan, the one for crazy people. They handcuffed her and dragged her out of the building and threw her in the back of their police unit.

This didn't make sense, and knowing the history of my family members butchering a familial event, I had to find out for myself. What had transpired? What had she done? What could a seventy-five-year-old woman have done to be pulled out of a nursing home and sent to a facility for the insane? Maybe she attacked an attendant. I could see that, but nothing that would elicit calling the cops. Throwing items at them, also very plausible, but that would be minor stuff.

I learned that nursing home attendants had called the deputy sheriff because Mom was uncontrollable, and the attendants could not restrain her. She was acting as if insane. A sudden change, they said. They believed she was drunk.

Two Newaygo County deputy sheriffs responded, with lights and sirens. They took Mom away in cuffs and in a squad car. They drove her four hours north to an insane asylum! Along the way, she quieted down. Records indicated she had slipped into a lethargic state. When they arrived at the state hospital, Mom was unresponsive.

With cursory conversation, the deputy sheriffs turned Mom over to white-uniformed male attendants.

They claimed she was drunk because they could smell alcohol under her breath. "A sweet smell," they said. To the credit of the attendants, once they heard she had a sweet breath smell, they knew what had happened, and quickly, quickly injected her with a saline/sugar concoction.

Mom let out a cry when they tried to sit her up. "My ribs! My ribs!"

It would be a day later that x-rays were be taken, but by then it was too late.

What the attendants at the nursing home failed to realize was that Mom had not been drinking but had been experiencing an insulin reaction. She apparently had not been getting a good diet with enough sugar in the food or drinks, leading to an imbalance of insulin in her blood. Too much insulin causes the breath to smell sweet, like ingested liquor. The attendants should have known this, but for some reason, they called the police instead.

The deputy sheriffs, relying on the testimony of the nursing home attendant, treated her as unruly and belligerent, throwing her in the back seat. That rough-housing broke several ribs. In transport, one broken rib punctured her right lung. Because of that, fluid had built up, and she developed pneumonia.

Mom could not catch a break. She lay in that circular bed, tubes in and out of her, dying. It was at that point that I sat with her for the last time. Other family members did not return to be at her side at her passing. Everyone had an excuse. Lack of transportation. Children for which to care, and no available babysitters. Live too far away. Car won't make it.

"No one to take me," one said, even though she was married.

"Can't get off work," said another.

"I can't stand to see her this way. I just can't take her suffering."

Lillian, Lorraine's twin, had married and moved away to the State of Washington, which relieved her of any familial duties. Mae, the eldest, had polio. Janet had found herself institutionalized in various facilities across Michigan. Janet's fraternal twin, Nellie, remained, but found herself incapable of taking the time to be there for Dad, despite living only thirty minutes away. Dad could no longer drive. He had his license taken away the year before when he was involved in his first car accident at age eighty-five. And it was a misnomer to call it an accident because a young man ran a four-way stop sign at the corner of Dayton and Elm, broadsiding Dad's old Chevy sedan as Dad was heading downtown to hang out with other Gerber retirees.

At the scene, the Fremont police officer admitted the other driver's fault and noted that Dad was eighty-five years old, precluding him from even operating a motor vehicle (that is just how the town worked back then). They took away Dad's license and condemned him to the whims of his selfish children's daily schedule, which would come to show that there were not enough hours in the day to get Dad to his appointments. Maybe once a month, one of the kids would find time to take him to the doctor to get his blood sugar tested. He grew weaker, unable to get uptown to commiserate with fellow retirees.

Dad sat in his favorite chair against the wall, smoking a pipe, hands folded behind his head. Quiet. Stoic. Zombie-like in a high-back wooden chair, he would sit . . . sit . . . waiting for lunch, which would not come with regularity any more now that "Aggie" was not there to make lunch. And there was no sense to eat, anyway. He wasn't going to sit at the table and look across at the chair now unoccupied. She wouldn't be eating her boiled egg, wheat toast, and black coffee with a smidgen of saccharin. They wouldn't be listening to the local news.

Lunch was exactly thirty minutes, the precise Dutch time, from 12:00 noon to 12:30 p.m. every day. After the obituary news aired, Mom and Dad would erect themselves from the kitchen table, clear dishes, and go do what old folks do when their purpose in life had changed to the social nub of things just around four walls and a tiny garden. Mom's raspberry patch had long since gone. Watering her tiger lilies was all he had left to do. But that took energy, and she wasn't there to opine about when they needed watering.

Dad made no effort to decide anything for Mom's funeral arrangements. What color coffin? What was her favorite dress? Her best church pendant? His kids bickered, realizing they were going to be inconvenienced with the sober funeral preparations. Mae, the eldest and happiest, knew of Mom's favorite hymns. They dressed her in her Sunday flowered dress and gold-colored necklace with sapphire stones, the only piece she had and had worn for years when Sunday came along.

All of Mom's fussing and fighting had ended. But for the daughters, Mom's passing gave them new cause for continued absences in helping Dad get through this. While the other siblings were picking out the plainest casket, Lorraine came to the house and sorted roughly through Mom's things. Dad sat in the high-back chair, hands folded behind his head, staring at nothing in particular, and possibly not uttering a word of protest.

Then came the funeral.

Lorraine wept the loudest, acting more as a paid mourner than one truly grieving. She was the belligerent in our family. The very daughter who had caused Mom so much unnecessary grief was now the most sorrow-struck, suffering adult child.

Mom and Dad had little money at the time of Mom's passing, so the funeral had to be plain. The funeral was small, with just family as congregants. Several Psalms were sung, the pastor of our church—who never really knew Mom—gave a generic eulogy, and then, with little fanfare, we headed to the cemetery, had a quick grave-yard service, and then a luncheon.

And with that, the existence of Mom was over.

35

BEAUTY IS THERAPY

A patch of strife, or a patch of joy,
it all depends on how you use it.

Anita Emery-De Visser

All her life, Mom expected a certain outcome from God, faithfully trusting. When those outcomes failed to materialize in her time, she became frustrated. Frustration led to puzzlement . . . then to hurt . . . then to outright anger. Then to war.

I watched Mom fight against things in life that were out of her control. She became consumed with what she could not change. It was as if she were chasing the wind or grasping at smoke. And in time, as she aged, the only thing in her control, she felt, was her small linear raspberry patch. And every late summer, her war with the neighbor kids ensued, which sadly, she never won. The kids ate her berries—berries she didn't want to pick, berries she didn't want to share. And that war stole her happiness. Caught up in her berry war, Mom lost sight of the fact that God had given her gifts. God's gifts were relationships, good food, sunny days, loving God—and berries.

It wasn't until her final days that I believe Mom finally realized one gift of God: our relationship. As Mom and I held hands at her deathbed, her focus was all on me. She controlled that moment and loved me. I loved her back, and in that moment, she won her last battle.

As for me, I must have faith that God has or will answer my prayers in His time. I should not focus on immediate outcomes outside my control, but have faith, and by faith, move though each day. In God's time, He will answer prayers.

I leave Mom in her resting place. I close that book. I am now an adult with children and grandchildren, but still molded and shaped by one Agnes Van der Weele De Visser.

I learned a patch of berries can be of strife, or a patch of berries can be of joy; it depends on how we use it. I will stop the raspberry wars, and if I ever raise raspberries, I will let kids eat from the vine as many as they want.

THE LORD'S VINEYARD

On that day
sing about a desirable vineyard:
I am the LORD, who watches over it
to water it regularly.
So that no one disturbs it,
I watch over it night and day.
I am not angry.
If only there were thorns and briers for me to battle,
I would trample them
and burn them to the ground.
Or let it take hold of my strength;
let it make peace with me—
make peace with me.
In days to come, Jacob will take root.
Israel will blossom and bloom
and fill the whole world with fruit.

(Isaiah 27:2–6 CSB)

FAMILY PHOTOS

Right: Agnes and Henry (right side) on their wedding day.

Below: Agnes as a teen.

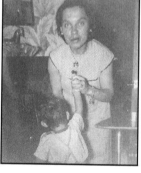

Above: The Leonard Vermeer family.

Above: Henry and Agnes.

Right: Sherwood with his biological mother, Janet.

Above: Sherwood with Mae.

Left: The happiest person in the world.

Left: Sherwood at the crippled children's camp.

Right: Sherwood age two, circa 1956.

285

ACKNOWLEDGMENTS

This, my first book, came into being because of my maternal grandparents, who not only took me in as one of their kids, but also, despite incredible social and physical disadvantages, gave me life when my biological mother was unable to care for me. My entire family is now gone, and they cannot enjoy the fruits of their labor, whether justified accolades or misdeeds—but all saved by grace. I offer up prayers for them for their obedience to raise me in the Reformed faith despite their human frailties.

A simple thank you will not suffice for many others. Without their valuable feedback, this book would have remained cluttered and disjointed in my head.

My deep thanks to:

Author Robert Hudson, for introducing me to Tisha Martin, my editor.

Tisha Martin, of Tisha Martin Editorial, LLC, my extraordinary editor. Without your guidance and encouragement, I would have given up.

Sarah Barnum, of TrailBlaze Editorial, for copy editing and typesetting and publishing assistance.

Sara Hemmeke, my illustrious illustrator whose sketches defined the tone of the work.

Ray Vander Weele, my chief advocate and sponsor.

The Van der Weeles, past and present generations,

for their love or angst with raspberries.

Jan Zwemer, preeminent Dutch historian of all things Dutch, Flemish, and of other outlier ancestry. The giving of your time for my project was humbling.

Thank you to the many others who contributed to this work, often in ways they might not even know:

Phil Deur, former police chief of Fremont, Michigan, for finding "Norma's" gravesite and cleaning it up. Because of your efforts, Norma will no longer be invisible.

Youth Pastor David Deur, for reading my first rough draft and sharing difficult epiphanies about the bullying we experienced as children.

Nancy Brookhouse, Dan Tibbets, Steven Lemanski, David T. Anderson, and my childhood belligerents in the Raspberry Wars, George Ranville, Jane Mendham, and Gary Zahrt.

Dan Gerber for sharing some family history for this project. Your assistance was appreciated.

And to "Suzie" at Crippled Children's Camp. I actually could not remember your name, but in that summer of 1960 at Hess Lake, Michigan, you gave me an emotional bridge back to health and a carefree childhood outlook. Wherever you are, God bless!

Special thanks to my wife, Anita Emery-De Visser, for your immense patience through the tough times in the writing of this book. Your profound insights were invaluable.

ABOUT THE AUTHOR

Sherwood De Visser's life transcends boredom. He survived high school and, with his parents' help, began working in several canneries in his hometown of Fremont, Michigan. Soon bored, he traveled "the World" during the Jesus Revolution era (1969–1972), hitchhiking out West, then to the Deep South, and on to New York state.

Innocently, he joined a Christian cult in Grass Valley, California, and later bootlegged liquor and beer for his brother-in-law in Mississippi. During his lifetime, Sherwood has held thirty-eight paid jobs, including a newspaper boy, an EMT, a paralegal, a teacher, and a professional investigator. He retired from private investigating in 2022.

He was accepted to Central Michigan University and graduated with bachelor's degrees in history and English. He holds a Provisional Certificate of Accomplishment in Education for Special Education from Eastern Michigan University.

Writing stemmed from his professors' encouragement. Sherwood received an honorable mention from the *Michigan Historical Review Journal for Dutch Ethnicity: A Study of a Benign Way of Life*. In 1983, he won the prestigious Cranbrook Grand Prize Award for Historical Fiction, for his short story, *Whiteman Shoes*. Guest author Orson Scott Card took him aside and said, "Your dialogue is as good as Ernest Hemmingway's. Keep on writing!"

Coming from such humble beginnings, Sherwood says, "I never would have pursued that path," if not for his English professors inspiring him to write.

Sherwood enjoys biking, tennis, and golf, and has been married to Anita for thirty-eight years. They reside in Michigan. *Raspberry Wars: My Boyhood through Berries, Bullying, and Bravery* is his first memoir. Visit www.sherwooddevisser.com.

ABOUT THE ILLUSTRATOR

Sara Hemmeke loves to bring joy to others through her art. Her creativity was evident as a child growing up in the Dutch subculture of West Michigan. She has a BFA in Graphic Design and has been a freelance artist for over twenty years. Along with illustration and design, she is a lettering artist and muralist. Sara is currently on the board of the Michigan Association of Calligraphers and an active volunteer in her community, bringing art to the public sphere. She and her husband, who is a pastor in the Reformed tradition, live in Howell, MI, with their four children. Visit www.sarahemmeke.com.

Made in the USA
Middletown, DE
24 September 2023

39049282R00163